A London policeman executes a tackle worthy of the rugby field, in the line of duty!

THE BOOK OF
DANGERMEN

Purnell

SBN 361 03886 0
Copyright © 1979 Purnell and Sons Limited
Published 1979 by Purnell Books, Berkshire House,
Queen Street, Maidenhead, Berkshire
Made and printed in Great Britain by Purnell and Sons
Limited, Paulton (Bristol) and London

Introduction

One dictionary gives the definition of 'brave' as meaning 'without fear'. This is certainly one interpretation, but is it altogether correct? Perhaps the bravest people are those who *do* know the meaning of fear, but who, in spite of that, face danger squarely in the face and conquer it.

Danger means different things to different people, but it is with us all, lurking in the corners of our lives to surprise us at any time. For some people—policemen, miners, firemen, lifeboatmen, and mountain rescue teams, amongst many—it is an intrinsic and accepted part of their daily work. If these people stopped working because they were in danger, society in its present form would cease functioning.

For others danger is something which is faced in their attempts to push back the frontiers of knowledge. The first men in space and on the Moon, test pilots flying prototype aircraft, deep-sea divers and scientists involved in dangerous nuclear research are people who experience the danger of the unknown.

But danger is eagerly sought by some people; it is the element which gives life excitement, interest, colour and spice. Motor-racing drivers, lone yachtsmen, mountaineers, jump jockeys and stuntmen are among those who thrill to the challenge of facing and overcoming danger. For people like these, danger is the very stuff of life.

This book shows you glimpses of the lives and work of some ordinary and extraordinary people. Reading it will excite you, chill you, sometimes horrify you and often make you laugh, but will never leave you in doubt about the sort of challenges which may one day come your way.

Contents

Danger —Part of the Job

Danger—Part of the Job
On Top of the World

These men (left) are all feeling on top of the world, with some of the best views of London spread before them.

Of course, it's no use taking this sort of job unless you have a good head for heights!

Perched on a tiny foothold on top of the Houses of Parliament are the three-man steeplejack team of Chick Segar, Vic Grealey and Jim Carey. It was a long climb, but that was the only way to remove the decorative crown for cleaning. The cameraman wasn't quite so brave: he climbed halfway up the flagpole, then used a remote-control lead to trigger the camera.

Ray Hume (below) gives a cheery wave as he surveys the best view in London. His crane was on top of the new National Westminster Bank tower block in the heart of the City of London. At 600ft it is the tallest solid structure in Britain, and the cab of Ray's crane was 30 feet above that. He needed

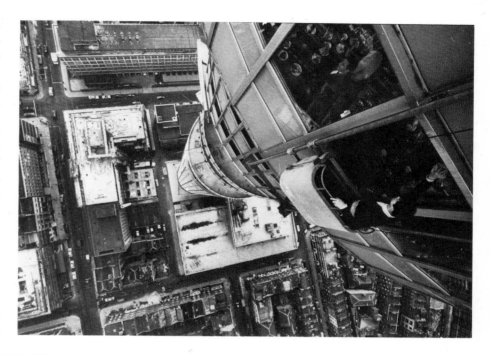

closed circuit television to watch the progress of the crane's loads.

Cleaning the windows of the Post Office tower (above) is another job which needs a steady head!

Danger—Part of the Job
Nerves of Steel

One of the loneliest jobs in the world is that of the bomb disposal man. There may be many people close by while he works. But for safety reasons they will all have been evacuated from the immediate area, and he is alone—with a bomb.

The only contact he has with other people is through his small radio which keeps him in touch with the team. A strict safety rule of "only one man at risk at any time" is enforced and so, all alone, our man will face the bomb. In many cases, everything will be unnaturally quiet and still; a bomb found in a busy shopping centre, for instance, will present a scene of total stillness and silence once the people have been evacuated, with, perhaps, a plastic cup blowing down the gutter making the only sound to be heard.

In others the scene is different, with an unnaturally high level of noise, as, for instance, working on a bomb in a telephone exchange. No incoming calls can be answered but people will still be trying to get through, unaware that the exchange is empty except for the technician—and the bomb.

During World War II the work of bomb disposal was shared between the Army, Navy and Air Force. Many medals were earned, sometimes posthumously. In peacetime, sad to say, bomb disposal is still needed to defuse bombs and explosive devices made by terrorists and this work is now carried out by Ammunition Technicians of the Royal Army Ordnance Corps.

The work is even more dangerous now than before. During the war, aircraft bombs were made to a set pattern. Each bomb of a particular type was likely to be the same as other bombs of that type. With terrorist devices, no two are quite the same.

The first task of the Ammunition Technician is to evaluate the situation and gather all the facts. A number of sophisticated aids are available to help him to diagnose what type of device he is dealing with. One of the most useful aids is the remote-controlled robot, which carries closed circuit television. Among the most dangerous situations are those in which the robot cannot be used.

But even when remote aids can be used, the technician has finally to go up to the bomb to make sure that it has been made safe.

Attitudes, some humorous, have been adopted by the Bomb Disposal men in relation to their task. The bomb is known as 'the dragon', and they speak of looking into the dragon's mouth, feeling the dragon's breath and so on. They have a code word for themselves: 'Felix'—the lucky black cat who walks alone and silently in the

Danger—Part of the Job

night, possessing the very necessary nine lives.

A Siamese cat once played a chancy part in a bomb disposal operation. A technician was working on the bomb in a small hotel. He had stopped the clockwork fuse and, with a long pole, had gently lifted the device and begun to place it into a sled which could then be drawn very gently into the street. As he raised the pole the bomb swung gently to and fro on the end. At that moment, down the stairs came a beautiful seal-pointed Siamese cat. Ignorant of the danger, he sat beneath the bomb patting it with his paws as it swung above his head!

If you talk to bomb disposal men you notice many contrasts in character and personality. But they all possess some qualities in common: they have the finest technical knowledge about ammunition and explosives, and they all possess patience, calmness and courage. They will all say that they take no chances. When they cannot predict with certainty the outcome of their next step they assume the worst and allow for it.

One thing on which they are adamant: the public should not touch any strange or suspicious objects which they find, but should call immediately upon the help of the police, who in turn will call on the services of the bomb disposal squad.

And another lonely operation will begin. . . .

Above: The first bomb of a new design which became known as the "Midlander". Right: A later version of the "Midlander"—no two devices are the same.

Left: A bomb on a petrol tanker exploded while the robot was examining it. The Ammunition Technician, whose life it undoubtedly saved, stands on the right.

9 March 1973: During a week of London bomb terror, this car bomb, planted near New Scotland Yard, was safely defused.

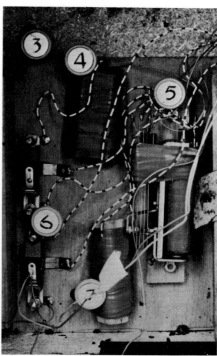

Danger—Part of the Job
The Atom • Friend and Foe

Research into nuclear energy has given Man the power to destroy himself completely. In 1945, two atomic bombs were dropped in Japan causing colossal damage. Hydrogen bombs could cause an even greater holocaust.

But, though research into nuclear energy is a highly dangerous business, physicists continue with it because of the enormous benefits that it could bring to mankind.

Plentiful power for ever and ever—that is what they promise us if they achieve their goal. They are moving towards a means of harnessing the same kind of process that enables the Sun and stars to keep on shining from millenium to millenium. That is, thermonuclear fusion.

In the interior of stars, at temperatures of tens of millions of degrees centigrade, hydrogen atoms combine with one another to form helium atoms. In so doing some of their mass is destroyed, reappearing as energy—heat and light—according to Albert Einstein's famous equation $E = mc^2$. The energy E equivalent to even a small mass m is stupendously high because of the presence of c in the equation, c being the velocity of light, which is 300,000 km/sec.

Man can already fuse hydrogen atoms in an uncontrolled way, and the result is the hydrogen bomb. The task of fusing hydrogen atoms in a controlled way is a lot more difficult, but not insurmountable. Predictions are that controlled fusion will be achieved within twenty years.

The exploitation of fusion still lies in the future, but the atom is already being put to good use. Since the 1950s electricity has been flowing from nuclear power stations throughout the world. These power stations harness energy produced by another type of atomic reaction—that of fission. In fission, heavy atoms like uranium are induced to split. In so doing their mass is destroyed, reappearing as energy according to Einstein's equation.

At present there are something like 200 nuclear power stations in 20 countries. In Britain $12\frac{1}{2}$ per cent of the electricity comes from

Left: Charging fuel into the reactor core at Hinkley 'B' nuclear power station. The power output from the twin-reactor station is 1,250,000 kilowatts. Fast reactors, like that at Dounreay (above), breed more fuel than they consume. Top right: Radioactive materials must be handled remotely in lead-lined chambers like this.

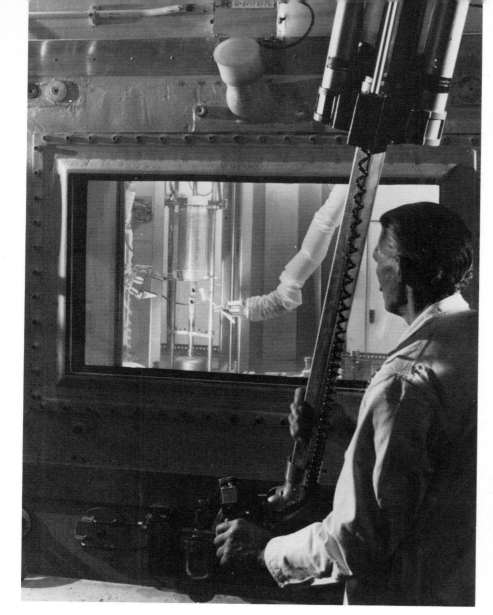

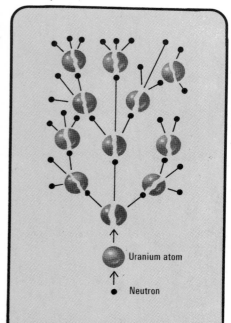

The rapid energy production from the fission of uranium atoms depends on a chain reaction. This reaction starts with the splitting of one atom by a neutron. This produces two or more other neutrons. They can split other atoms, which in turn can split still more atoms. Energy is given out at each fission.

nuclear stations, but in America, now the biggest nuclear electric producer, the figure is less than one per cent. Nuclear plants also power many submarines and a few surface ships.

The heart of the nuclear power plant is the reactor, where nuclear fission takes place continuously by a chain reaction in which neutrons produced from one fission cause other fissions. Control is exercised over the process by inserting in the reactors rods that absorb neutrons. The control rods are pushed in or pulled out as necessary to keep the fission process 'ticking over'.

There are many potential hazards associated with a nuclear plant and stringent precautions are taken to eliminate them. One is that the chain reaction will get out of control and create a catastrophic

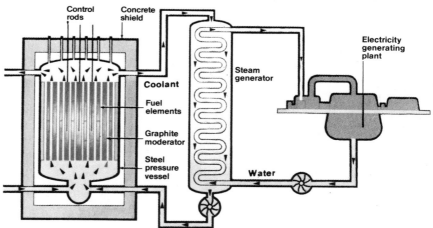

explosion. This is prevented by making all the controls fail-safe: if a defect occurs in the plant, the control rods are quickly pushed fully home and the reactor is shut down. The chances against a reactor turning into an atomic bomb are about a million to one.

The principle behind nuclear power generation. Fission takes place in the uranium fuel of the reactor core. Graphite is needed to assist the fission process. A coolant passes on the heat produced in the core to water in the generator, thus turning it into steam. This is subsequently fed to turbo-generators to produce electricity.

Danger—Part of the Job
Radiation

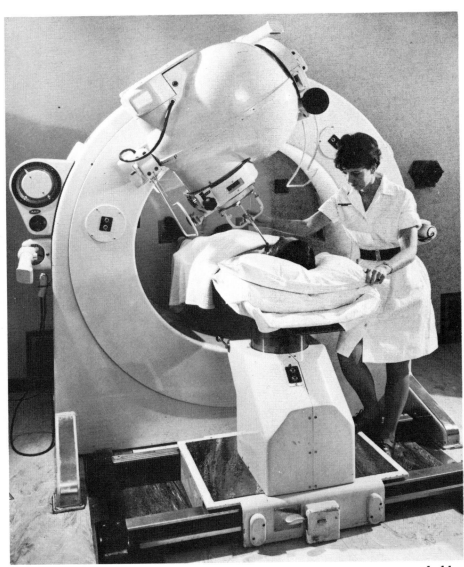

This is a heart pacemaker powered by an atomic battery. Some people need a pacemaker to stimulate their heart to beat properly. It is surgically implanted in the chest, and needs replacing when the battery runs down. Atomic batteries are better because they last for years.

One of the major problems of atomic energy is that of radiation. Uranium and the products that result from its fission are highly radioactive, emitting harmful radiation that is unseen and penetrating. Unless they are protected, workers in an atomic plant might suffer burns, sickness and even death from the radiation. Also they might suffer genetic damage, so that their offspring could be affected.

To prevent this from happening, nuclear reactors are surrounded by a thick steel and concrete biological shield. All workers handle radioactive material from a distance and in shielded enclosures, working by remote control. Automatic detection devices are located throughout nuclear establishments to monitor radioactivity levels and warn if they become too high. All the people working there wear lapel badges called 'dosimeters'. The dosimeters are checked regularly to ensure that the permitted

Danger—Part of the Job

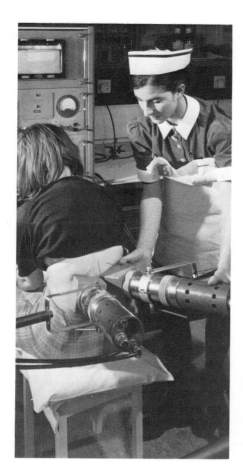

fusion. Unlike fission, there are few hazards associated with fusion because the product—helium—is not radioactive. And there are no other harmful wastes.

In industry and medicine, radiation devices are being ever more widely used, all the while increasing the radiation risk. The commonest, of course, are X-ray machines. The slight dose needed to X-ray a person is quite harmless. But the operators of the machines must take precautions from excessive exposure by wearing protective clothing. So must the operators of radio-therapy machines which expose patients to the radiation of radioactive materials such as radium. Here the radiation is deliberately focused on the patient, for example, to kill cancerous growths before they spread.

The hazards of exposure to radiation were tragically demonstrated by the survivors of the Hiroshima and Nagasaki atomic bombs. Many of them died long afterwards of leukemia, a disease of the blood-producing organs. This is the same disease that killed Marie Curie, who discovered and isolated the highly radioactive element radium. It is probable that Marie, winner of two Nobel prizes (1903 and 1911) for her work, was the first radiation victim.

radiation dose is never exceeded.

For these reasons, nuclear research establishments are not dangerous places to work. It is the potential rather than the actual threat that remains in the mind.

A greater drawback than radiation is waste disposal. The products resulting from fission are highly radioactive and only part can be used again. Disposal of the rest is a problem, because it will stay radioactive for tens of thousands of years. Some of this deadly waste has been sealed in drums and sunk in deep ocean trenches; some is stored above ground under constant guard. But it is this problem that threatens to restrict the further development of fission reactors. Waste from the second generation reactors—the fast reactors—is even more deadly because it contains large amounts of plutonium which is used in nuclear weapons.

The solution to this would be a breakthrough in thermonuclear

Danger—Part of the Job
London's Firefighters

Right: A crew wearing breathing apparatus. Far right: A fire at a London nurses' home in 1976. Crews are on the roof and turntable ladders are in use.

Below: A hotel guest is assisted down an extension ladder by a member of the Brigade during a fire. Note the method of holding the man *on to* the ladder.

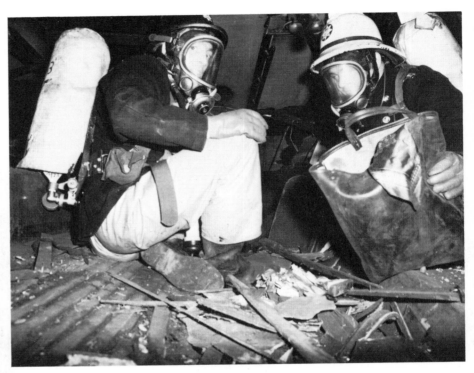

In the past ten years, 1118 firemen of London's Fire Brigade have been injured, and nine killed. Multiply these figures to cover fire brigades throughout the country, and you have some idea of the dangers which the firemen face.

When the alarm bell goes, the firemen do not know whether they are being called to a small fire or a major conflagration. Of course, they prefer to tackle fires before they get out of hand, because then the danger to their own lives and the lives of other people is much less.

Firefighting today is a highly organised business, with emergency calls being routed to a well-equipped control room where an operator can use computers and teleprinters to pinpoint the exact location of the fire and call out the Brigade in a matter of seconds.

But it was not always like that. In 1600 the first primitive fire appliances made their appearance in England. They were mainly big syringes (known as fire squirts), or manually operated pumps mounted on a tank of water with a nozzle on the top.

They were not very effective, however, and in 1666 the Great Fire devastated London. There was little equipment available to fight the fire, and much of that did not work. Water for firefighting had to be brought from the river.

After this major disaster, the insurance companies formed their own firefighting brigades. Everyone who paid for the insurance was issued with a metal badge to place on the front of his house. When a house caught fire the fire brigades would rush to the scene, but would refuse to fight the fire if their own badge was not displayed outside.

Companies pooled their resources to form the London Fire

Danger—Part of the Job

Engine establishment, which laid the foundations of the London Fire Brigade as we know it today.

Run by the Greater London Council, it has 11 divisions and employs 6500 men using 500 fire fighting appliances. In London alone, over 100,000 calls are dealt with each year, about one-third of them being to emergencies such as road, rail and aircraft crashes, floods or people trapped in lifts.

Great importance is attached to fire prevention, and the Fire Brigades spend much of their time advising on fire precautions and inspecting hotels and boarding houses to ensure that the fire precautions are adequate.

The firemen have to be trained to cope with every conceivable type of situation, from a chemical incident in a factory to fires in theatres and clubs, on the London Underground system or to shipping on the Thames. There is a special river service which copes with about 600 calls a year.

The highly skilled men of the fire service are on call every day, 24 hours a day, and they risk their lives countless times a year. To them, it is all part of the day's work.

Royal Firefighter

King Edward VII, when Prince of Wales, took a keen personal interest in the business of fire fighting.

His uniform was always kept at the ready at the Chandos Street fire station, so that he could attend the more notable fires.

Into Space

Man on the Moon

Man has performed many feats of daring, courage and endurance during his relatively short lifetime on this planet, for he is fascinated by the unknown, and lured towards it.

This lure tempted Christopher Columbus to the New World; Captain Cook to the southern continent; Scott and Amundsen to the South Pole. And on 12 April 1961 it led Yuri Gagarin into space.

The astonishing thing about the historic first orbital flight by Russian cosmonaut Gagarin was that

it occurred so soon after the first ever launching into space—that of Sputnik 1 in October 1957. A few months after Gagarin, cosmonaut Gherman Titov became the second spaceman to go into orbit. Not until February 1962 did the first American venture into orbit—astronaut John Glenn.

Spurred by national pride and strategic implications, a space race developed between the world's two giant nations. President Kennedy promised to put an American on the Moon by the end of the decade. At first the Russians led the race,

Above: Cosmonaut Yuri Gagarin, who was the first man to orbit the Earth, in 1961. He was born at Gzhatsk, near Moscow, in 1934. He was killed in an air crash only seven years after his historic space flight.

Left: Apollo 16 astronaut David Scott, snapped by his fellow Moonwalker James Irwin on their visit to the Sea of Rains in 1971. In the background are the foothills of the lunar Apennine mountain range.

Far left: 1973: On a mock-up of the space station Skylab, a space flight centre technician checks the procedures to be used to raise a 'sunshade' to cool the crippled Skylab, currently orbiting the Earth.

Into Space

This diagram outlines the method Apollo astronauts used to reach the Moon. Their spacecraft was made up of three parts, or modules. Two astronauts descended to the Moon's surface in the lunar module.

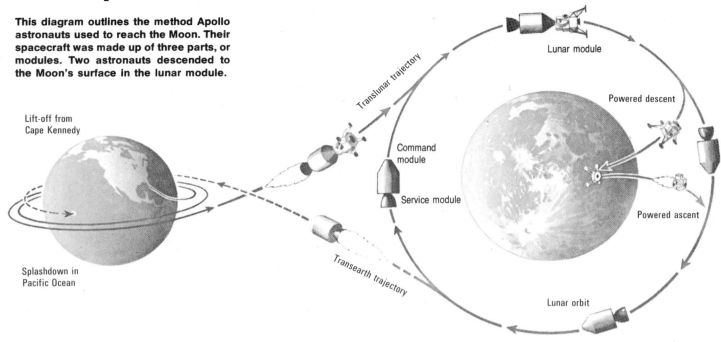

Lift-off from Cape Kennedy

Splashdown in Pacific Ocean

Translunar trajectory

Command module

Service module

Transearth trajectory

Lunar module

Powered descent

Powered ascent

Lunar orbit

Nowadays spacewalks, or EVA's, are commonplace, but until 1965 no one had dared to leave the comparative safety of their spacecraft. In March of that year cosmonaut Alexei Leonov made the first space walk, drifting for some 20 minutes outside his Voshkod craft. Three months later Edward White made the first American walk in space (above), from a Gemini 4 craft. He was killed two years later in a fire while training for the Apollo missions.

launching the first two- and three-man craft, Voshkod, and the first woman into space, Valentina Tereshkova, in 1963. Two years later, cosmonaut Alexei Leonov performed the first ever space walk in Earth orbit.

But by then American know-how and capital investment had begun to pay off. The two-man Gemini flights proved spectacularly successful, and set the stage for the three-man Apollo flights that were to follow. The Apollo project had its sights on the Moon. The 1968 circumnavigation of the Moon by Apollo 8 showed that the US was capable of achieving its goal. Astronauts James Lovell, William Anders and Frank Borman became the first of a new breed of true spacemen, who travelled far from their home planet. For six days their home was a flimsy capsule a few metres across. Had their spacecraft developed serious trouble or radio links with Earth failed, they would have been completely beyond help, doomed to drift for ever in the black void of space.

On 20 July 1969 came another historic moment when Apollo 11's Moon lander Eagle touched down on the lunar surface. A few hours later astronaut Neil Armstrong made what he called "a small step for a man, a giant leap for mankind" and planted the first human footprint in the lunar soil. He and fellow astronaut Edwin Aldrin unveiled a plaque on the descent stage of the lunar lander that recorded for posterity a milestone in Man's history: 'Here men from planet Earth first set foot on the Moon, July 1969 AD. We came in peace for all mankind.'

Between then and December 1972 five more teams of courageous astronauts voyaged to the Moon and landed. In all they spent 166 hours exploring the Moon's surface, on foot and latterly by moon buggy. They collected 385 kg (850 lb) of rock and soil samples and set up remote-controlled scientific sta-

tions at each launching site.

The cost of the greatest adventure of all time? About $25,000 million. Whether it was worth it is a matter for debate. Man being Man, sooner or later someone would have gone to the Moon because it represents a challenge, a cosmic Everest, to be climbed 'because it's there'.

Right: The Moon now bears the footprints of 12 American astronauts, who landed on it between July 1969 and December 1972. They show up clearly in the dusty surface.

Below: The $13 million lunar roving vehicle, or moon buggy, used on the last three Apollo missions. It had four-wheel electric drive and had a top speed of about 15 kilometres per hour.

Into Space

Living in Space

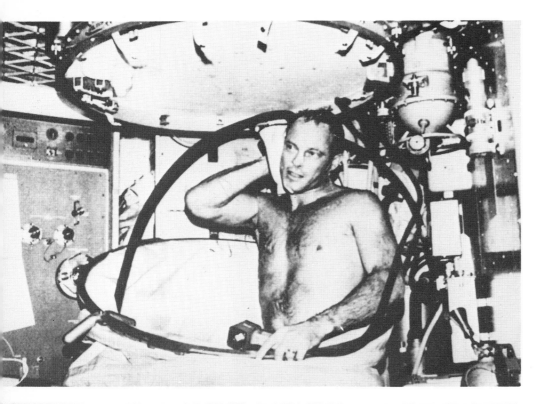

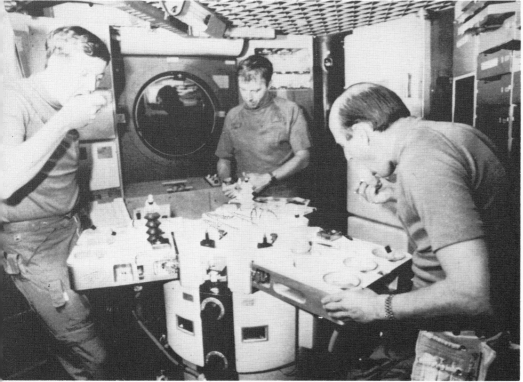

Space is an extremely hostile environment for Man. On Earth he is cocooned by the atmosphere. It supplies him with air, which contains the oxygen he must breathe to stay alive. It acts as an insulating blanket to prevent him becoming too hot or too cold. It also filters out harmful rays from the Sun. So when Man ventures into space he must take a replica of the atmosphere with him.

Providing a suitable atmosphere is the main task of a spacecraft's life-support system. This system provides a mixture of oxygen and nitrogen, often at a somewhat lower pressure than the atmosphere, rather as in a pressurized aircraft. It incorporates a very efficient air conditioner which removes the exhaled carbon dioxide from the air, together with any odours. It also regulates the temperature and humidity of the artificial atmosphere.

When an astronaut needs to leave his craft in space, he dons a spacesuit which is plumbed into the spacecraft's life-support system via a so-called umbilical cord. This cord not only provides the astronaut with oxygen; it also pipes water through his underwear to keep him cool. For safety's sake, he also carries an emergency oxygen supply. The outer suit the astronaut wears on top of the pressure garment is multi-layered and aluminized to provide insulation and reflect radiation. It also provides protection against impact by tiny meteoroids, or cosmic dust particles. The space helmet has a visor to protect the eyes.

Another aspect of life support is the obvious one of providing orbiting astronauts with food and drink. Some of their foods are dehydrated to save weight and to preserve

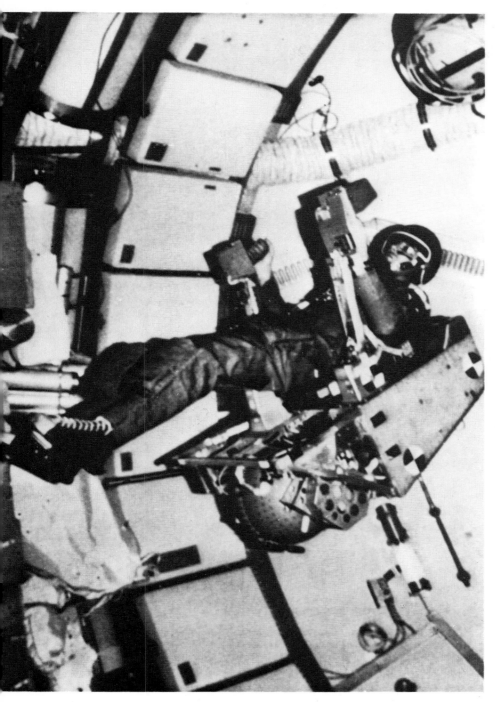

cottage cheese, black currant jam and cream, and tea. *Chez* Apollo, they dined on fish soup with mushrooms, steak, grapefruit juice, strawberries, pears and apricots.

The condition astronauts find most difficult to cope with is weightlessness, or the lack of gravity. In orbit there is nothing to keep their feet 'on the ground'; there is no 'up' or 'down'. They cannot walk properly, but have to float everywhere using their hands and feet to pull or push their bodies along. If they want to sit or stand still, they must strap their feet down. When they go to bed, they must zip themselves into sleeping bags which are usually attached to the walls.

Conventional hygiene methods are also out, for they would result in drops of water, shaving cream, toothpaste and whiskers escaping into the cabin air. So a wipe-down with damp towels does for washing, and shaving is done with vacuum electric shavers. Occasional showers may be taken, inside a tent fitted with a vacuum water collector. Going to the toilet in no-gravity conditions, if you think about it, also presents problems. So again vacuum devices are employed to remove the wastes.

Living in space, then, is different, but Man, a very adaptable creature, copes with it well. The lengthy Skylab and Salyut orbital experiments (see page 26) have proved that. The two things that space scientists thought might prevent Man remaining for long in space—radiation and weightlessness—have not proved stumbling blocks after all. We already have had our first space baby, Elena (born 1964), a perfectly healthy offspring of Soviet cosmonauts Valentina Tereshkova and Andrian Nikolayev. Valentina says she received a smaller dose of radiation on her space trip than during a routine chest X-ray. So there was absolutely no risk of space radiation-induced genetic defects occurring in her children.

Above: A large compartment in Skylab provided astronauts with sufficient room to carry out various experiments with this jet manoeuvring unit.

Top left: The Skylab astronauts were the first to sample the luxury of a space shower. Jack Lousma is seen clearly enjoying one here.

Left: Skylab astronauts, seen here in training, were also the first to enjoy a varied and appetising menu 'just like real home cooking'.

them. They have to be mixed with water and kneaded inside their container tubes before eating. Other foods are supplied in tins or are deep frozen. The menus are not as spartan as one might think. On the joint Apollo-Soyuz flight in 1975, the American astronauts and Russian cosmonauts who linked up in space dined *chez* Soyuz on Slichi (cabbage soup), tongue, rye bread and honey cakes, prunes and nuts,

Into Space and Back

Though living in orbit is not without its hazards, the most dangerous periods of space missions are launching and re-entry, that is, getting into and returning from space. Astronauts ride into space in a tiny capsule perched on a rocket containing hundreds of thousands of litres of highly explosive fuel—liquid hydrogen, kerosene and liquid oxygen. When ignited the fuel burns, producing a flaming jet of gases that propels the rocket by reaction. The acceleration is tremendous, and astronauts are pressed back in their seats with three or four times the force of gravity. They must lie with their backs towards the thrust to reduce the risk of their blacking out or causing damage to their internal organs.

As the rocket gathers speed, its various stages run out of fuel and fall away. Within minutes the astronauts in their spacecraft are in orbit, travelling at some 28,000 km/h (17,500 mph). The whole launching sequence is under the automatic control of computers, which instantly make corrections to course, thrust and so on, in response to signals from sensors in the inertial guidance and other systems. No human being could react swiftly enough to control the launching sequence. To allow for things going wrong during launch, the astronauts' capsule is sited at the tip of the launching vehicle, and is fitted with an independent escape rocket, rather like an aeroplane's ejection seat, for rapid emergency escapes.

Returning from space is, if anything, even more hazardous. The spacecraft must be slowed down from orbital speed (28,000 km/h) to a few kilometres an hour to ensure a safe, soft landing for the astronauts. The first step is to fire the retro-rockets in the direction in which the craft is travelling. This slows it down to below orbital speed. It drops from orbit and re-enters the atmosphere. Immediately, it begins to slow down and heat up because of air friction, but

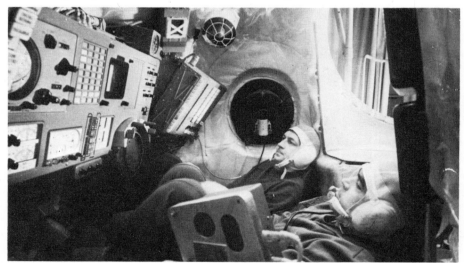

Left: A Soyuz spacecraft, with two cosmonauts on board, accelerates off the launching pad at Baikonur Cosmodrome. Above: Cosmonauts train in a simulator for their forthcoming flight. Top right: Much travelled cosmonaut Alexei Leonov is here seen practising emergency escape procedures.

entry; only the crew module returns to Earth intact.

The early history of Soyuz is not a happy one and emphasises the dangers inherent in any space flight.

The first known space casualty, cosmonaut Vladimir Komarov, met his death while returning from the first Soyuz flight. The landing parachute got tangled up, and the descent capsule smashed into the ground at high speed. After a highly successful 24-day mission in Soyuz 11, in which they docked with the first Salyut space station, Russian cosmonauts Vladislav Volkov, Viktor Patsayev and Georgy Dobrovolsky were found to be dead when their capsule touched down on Earth. The capsule had sprung a leak half an hour previously and they had been killed instantly by the sudden depressurization.

Like children the whole world over, these Russians dream of flying into space. They belong to Leningrad's Young Cosmonauts Club. There they learn about the principles, practice and problems of space flight, about astronomy, and many other things. One day some of them may well achieve their dream and become cosmonauts.

the plastic heat shield on the outside protects the astronauts on the inside from being cooked to a cinder. During this phase, no signals can get to or from the craft, because the ionized air around the craft blocks them.

The resistance of the atmosphere continues to slow down the returning spacecraft until at about 10,000 metres (33,000 ft) parachutes open to slow it down further for a soft landing. To date all returning American spacecraft—the Mercury, Gemini and Apollo—have splashed down at sea near a recovery ship. By contrast Russian craft are designed to touch down on land. To make sure of a very soft landing, they are fitted with additional retro-rockets which the cosmonauts are able to fire as they approach the ground.

From 1979 all American manned space launchings will take place in a new generation of space vehicle—the Space Shuttle (see page 28). This is the space transportation system of the future. The Russians are also considering a shuttle system, but it appears likely that their present Soyuz spacecraft will continue to be their standard launch vehicle for some years. The Soyuz craft is about 7 m (23 ft) long and is made up of three sections, or modules. The crew journeys to and from space in a spherical descent module. In orbit they live and work in the larger orbital module, at the rear of which is the instrument or service module. The orbital and instrument modules are jettisoned before re-

Into Space

Space Stations

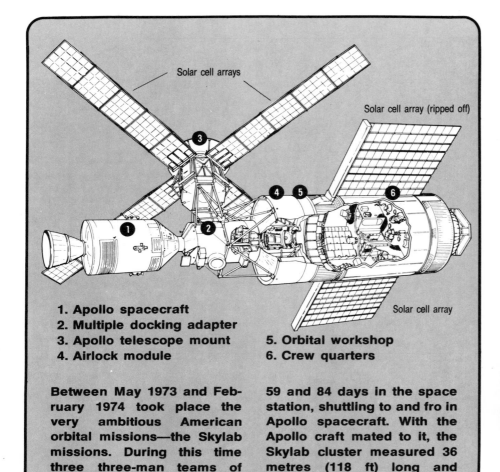

1. Apollo spacecraft
2. Multiple docking adapter
3. Apollo telescope mount
4. Airlock module
5. Orbital workshop
6. Crew quarters

Between May 1973 and February 1974 took place the very ambitious American orbital missions—the Skylab missions. During this time three three-man teams of astronauts spent in turn 28, 59 and 84 days in the space station, shuttling to and fro in Apollo spacecraft. With the Apollo craft mated to it, the Skylab cluster measured 36 metres (118 ft) long and weighed 90,000 tonnes.

extended periods.

The highly successful Skylab project came about because there was surplus hardware left over from the Apollo Moon programme, in particular a huge Saturn V rocket. This powerful launching vehicle made it possible to launch a heavy, ready-made station into orbit. This station was a surplus rocket casing that had been elaborately converted and equipped.

During their extended stays in space the Salyut and Skylab astronauts have conducted hundreds of experiments in many scientific fields. Their craft have been equipped with elaborate instrumentation to study both the near-Earth and the deep-space environment. The Skylab astronauts in

The Russians launched the first orbiting space station in 1971, called Salyut.

By mid-1978 six Salyut craft had been launched into orbit. They had been visited by two-man teams of cosmonauts, ferried to and fro by Soyuz spacecraft. The Soyuz 8 crew, Pyotr Klimuk and Vitali Sevastyanov, spent 63 days working in Salyut 4 in 1975. The Soyuz 27 crew, Yuri Romanenko and Georgi Grechko, spent 96 days aboard Salyut 6, landing in March 1978.

Two notable events occurred during the Salyut 6 mission. The space station was visited by an automatic freight carrier, Progress I, carrying fresh fuel and supplies. The first triple link-up between manned spacecraft occurred between Soyuz 28 and the Salyut 6—Soyuz 27 complex.

The Salyut 6 mission exceeded in length by 12 days that of Skylab 3, the third visit to the American Skylab space station in 1973/4. Whereas Skylab was a 'one-off' job, the Salyut missions will continue at least for the time being. But plans are already afoot, so Russian space experts say, for the building of stations much bigger than Salyut which will accommodate crews of up to 20 people for

particular concentrated on studying the Sun and accumulated more data on it than the hundreds of Earth-based solar observers could have done in a century. Many engineering techniques have been investigated, too, such as welding and soldering metals and growing ultra-pure crystals.

The astronauts have carried out numerous medical and biological experiments. The behaviour of insects, spiders, fish and plants, bacteria and other micro-organisms has been investigated in the space environment. Plants have been cultivated in mini-greenhouses as a step towards in-orbit horticulture, which could provide fresh vegetables on long space missions. A start has been made, too, in Salyut experiments, to recy-

Left: A young girl testing one of the units of the reusable space laboratory Spacelab. Below: This picture illustrates the moment just before docking between Soyuz and Salyut craft.

cle the material astronauts consume. Recycling will ultimately be necessary to conserve the limited resources of space stations and make them partially independent of Earth.

In the 1980s astronaut-engineers will be launched into space with a different purpose—to build large and permanently manned space stations. The first ones will be made by linking together modules ferried into space by the Space Shuttle. NASA's proposed Manned Orbital Facility, for example, is one such scheme. The basic station will consist of four main units—a subsystem module for power, communication and control equipment; a logistics module which contains cargo, stores and additional living space; a habitability module, which provides sleeping, eating and recreational facilities; and a payload module, which contains the experimental equipment. Additional units could be added later to expand the station. Such stations will also act as a base for other space constructions. These will include huge radio telescopes for studying the universe, and power satellites to collect and beam solar power to Earth.

Looking into the next century, the most far-sighted space scientists, like Gerald O'Neill of Princeton University, suggest that space colonies will be established. They will be built in orbit, 350,000 km distant. They will be constructed from materials mined at bases on the Moon, from where they will be shot into space by an ingenious electromagnetic catapult.

If this kind of scheme, envisaged for a century hence, sounds fantastic now, so a century ago did the idea of Man landing on the Moon. Will Man colonize space? Will he travel to the planets? Will he ultimately reach the stars? The answer must be 'yes'. There are bound to be disasters along the way, but, as Yuri Gagarin said when learning of Vladimir Komarov's death: "Nothing can stop us!"

Into Space

Space Shuttle

The Space Shuttle seems set to pioneer a new era in space transportation—one in which ordinary men and women may one day participate. The illustration shows the configuration of the Shuttle system at launching. The wing orbiter rides into space attached to its massive fuel tank and twin rocket boosters. It drops these before it soars into orbit. On completing its mission, it drops from orbit and lands like a plane on an ordinary runway.

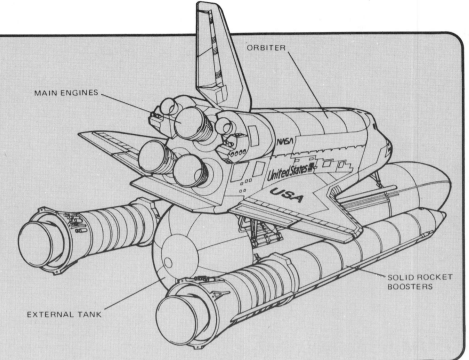

ORBITER

MAIN ENGINES

SOLID ROCKET BOOSTERS

EXTERNAL TANK

At present space launchings are incredibly expensive. The trouble is that the rockets used to launch spacecraft can be used only once. They thrust the spacecraft into orbit and then either end up in the sea, burn up in the atmosphere, or remain in orbit as so much space flotsam. The spacecraft, too, can be used only once, and if it develops a malfunction, it must be written off.

By 1980, however, all that will be changed—by the advent of the Space Shuttle, which is a re-usable craft. Apart from the main fuel tank, all of the Shuttle is designed for re-use up to 100 times. All the Shuttles will be manned, and the crew will have the capability not only of launching satellites, but also of retrieving or servicing satellites already in orbit. With the cost of satellites running into tens of millions of dollars, the advantage of retrieval and re-use is only too apparent.

The Shuttle, for satellite launching flights, would have a crew of

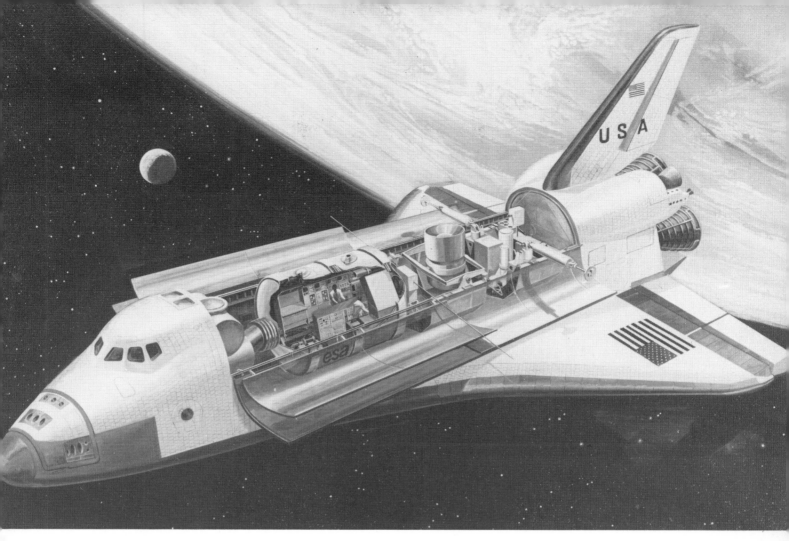

Above: The Space Shuttle in orbit, some 500 km above the Earth. Its cargo bay doors are open, showing its payload—Spacelab. Spacelab consists of a pressurized laboratory unit, in which scientists work, and an instrument pallet, open to space.

Far left: An orbiter under construction. It is built mainly of aluminium alloy, covered by heat-resistant material.

only three—the pilot, co-pilot and a payload specialist.

For more complex missions, such as Spacelab, it can accommodate a further four people. Unlike the space travellers of today these people will not have to be very highly trained astronauts. They will not wear spacesuits or need to know how to fly the Shuttle. They will, of course, have to undergo certain training to prepare them for weightlessness, for example, and they must be experts in the experimental fields currently being investigated in the space environment.

At last ordinary men—and women—will be able to travel in space, ushering in a new era in space travel. In the foreseeable future it seems quite probable that passenger travel into orbit will become a reality.

The main part of the Shuttle system is the delta-winged orbiter, which carries crew and payload. The orbiter, which is a cross between a plane and a rocket, is about the same size as a medium-range jet airliner like the DC-9 or the Trident. It is 37 metres (122 ft) long, and has a wing span of 24 metres (78 ft). At launch it sits on a much bigger main fuel tank, to the sides of which are attached booster rockets. Its rocket engines and the boosters all fire at lift-off.

When their fuel is spent, the boosters parachute back to Earth and are recovered to be used again. Minutes later, the main fuel tank empties and is jettisoned, while the orbiter continues into orbit. When its mission is completed, it fires retro-rockets that slow it down,

and it re-enters the atmosphere. It glides in to land on a runway, like a plane, though somewhat faster.

The crew members are housed in a triple-deck pressurized crew module in the front of the fuselage. The bulk of the craft, however, comprises the cargo bay, which is some 18 metres (60 ft) long and $4\frac{1}{2}$ metres (15 ft) in diameter. One of the main payloads for the Shuttle will be Spacelab, which has been designed and built by the European Space Agency to fit the cargo bay. Spacelab consists of a pressurized module, where four specialist scientists will carry out their experiments. Another module will be open to expose instruments directly to the space environment.

It is certain that in the 1980s the Shuttle will start lifting into orbit parts that will be assembled into near-Earth space stations, which will be permanently manned. The building of such structures represents the next stage in Man's conquest of space.

Space 'Records'

The First Moon Walk

The first man on the Moon was 39-year-old Neil Armstrong, command pilot of the Apollo II mission, the US space odyssey. Armstrong stepped off the space craft on to the surface of the Moon's Sea of Tranquillity at 02.56 hours and 15 seconds Greenwich Mean Time on 21 July 1969. He was followed out of the Lunar Module *Eagle* by Colonel Edwin Aldrin Jr. while Lt. Col. Michael Collins orbited above them in the Command Module *Columbia*.

Apollo II had blasted off from Cape Kennedy at 13.32 GMT on 16 July and landed on the Moon at 20.17 and 42 seconds GMT on 20 July.

The First Death

The dubious distinction of being the first astronaut to be killed in space goes to the Russian Colonel Vladimir Komarov. He was launched in the spacecraft Soyuz on 23 April 1967, and was in orbit for about $2\frac{1}{2}$ hours. On final descent the parachute failed and he was killed.

The First Flight

The first successful flight beyond the Earth's atmosphere was by the Russian cosmonaut Yuri Gagarin on 12 April 1961. He completed a single orbit of the Earth in Vostok 1 in 89.34 minutes. The whole flight took only 108 minutes, but it proved that man could become used to weightlessness and could control instruments while in space. It also proved that he could withstand the launch and return safely to the surface of the Earth. Gagarin was killed in a plane crash near Moscow on 27 March 1968.

The First 'Century'

On 21 September 1978 two Russian cosmonauts became the first space travellers to spend 100 days in orbit. They were Vladimir Kovalyonok and Alexander Ivanchenkov, in the space station Salyut 6—Soyuz 31. During this first space 'century' the two cosmonauts circled the Earth 1600 times and travelled a distance of more than 65 million kilometres. Salyut 6 was then by far the most visited spacecraft in the history of space travel.

Russian Valentina Tereshkova, who in 1963 was the first woman to journey into space.

The Highest

The greatest altitude so far attained by man was by the crew of the ill-fated Apollo 13 who on 15 April 1970 were a mind-boggling 248,655 miles *above* the Earth's surface. The crew comprised Captain James Lovell, Frederick Haise Jr. and John Swigert Jr.

The Fastest

The fastest speed at which any man has travelled was achieved by the Command Module of Apollo 10, carrying Col. Thomas Stafford and Commanders Gene Cernan and John Young. It reached a speed of 24,791 mph on its trans-Earth return flight on 26 May 1969.

The First Space Walk

The first man to 'walk' in space was the Russian Lt. Col. Aleksey Leonov. He left the Russian satellite Voshkod on 18 March 1965 and was 'in space' for about 20 minutes.

Screen Stuntmen

The Specialists

When a film script demands high risk action, the services of a highly skilled stuntman will be employed to provide the thrills and spills. Often he will 'double' for the film's star when the action gets too tough. He is paid to take risks. He will set fire to himself, crash a car at high speed, dive off a cliff, fall off a galloping horse or leap from a speeding train. He will 'die' countless times.

The men and women who make their living out of stunt work are highly trained specialists. In most cases they earn their reputations by concentrating on one particular type of stunt—so there is the high-fall specialist; the car stunt artist; the horse stunt action man.

The stunt performers will be part of a team during the filming of a dangerous action sequence. The team, master-minded by a Stunt Co-ordinator, will work closely with the film's director.

Stunts are planned meticulously, safety always being of prime importance. But accidents do happen, and men have lost their lives performing dangerous stunts.

Some of the most exciting sequences in modern films are those involving cars. Hardly a film comes to the screen these days without a spectacular car chase such as the breathtaking scenes in the Steve McQueen film *Bullitt*. McQueen himself did some of the stunt work, but he worked closely with seven of Hollywood's most daring car stunt artists headed by stunt co-ordinator Carey Loftin.

Another top 'car specialist' is Remy Julienne whose work was seen to its best advantage in *The Italian Job*, starring Michael Caine. For one thrilling sequence three cars—Minis—were seen leaping simultaneously 50 feet in

Would you leap 105 feet from a grain elevator, to land on an airbag 18 feet by 24 feet, and only 8 feet deep? That is what stuntman Dar Robinson did for the film *Stunts*. He wore no special protection, relying entirely on the way he landed to protect himself.

The pictures show him just after leaping from the high building, and then halfway down. In the picture above you can see the airbag which will soften his landing, and the cameraman crouched behind it, filming the jump.

33

Screen Stuntmen

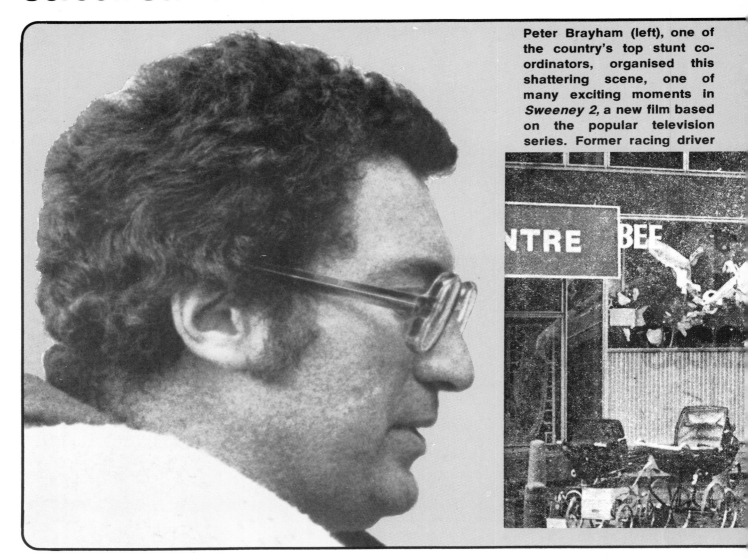

Peter Brayham (left), one of the country's top stunt co-ordinators, organised this shattering scene, one of many exciting moments in *Sweeney 2,* a new film based on the popular television series. Former racing driver

the air from one rooftop to another, across a 42-foot gap.

Before filming took place, intensive preparations were carried out to make sure the stunt would work. On a deserted, unfinished road in Turin (the setting of the film), run-up lengths were measured and take-off ramps were angled and tested. Practice jumps of gradually increasing lengths were carried out. For the actual filming, the cars took off at 57 mph after an approach run of 30 yards. Not only did they clear the gap, but also the reception ramp designed to bring them gently down.

"The moment of danger is very short—a few seconds—but the danger, while it lasts, is very big," said Remy. "There is always a

Frank Henson, an old hand at car-crashing stunts for the camera, was at the wheel of the car. Not content with smashing through the plate-glass of this shopping centre, Frank then crash-landed and made a quick getaway!

point of no return."

The most breathtaking car stunt ever performed in London must surely have been one which involved car stuntman Peter Brayham in the John Wayne film *Brannigan*.

Peter, one of Britain's leading stunt co-ordinators, whose work can also be seen in the TV and big screen versions of *The Sweeney*, did

Left: A hair-raising scene from *Stunts*, a film which uncovers the thrilling world of stunts and stuntmen. Bud Davis, pictured here, was dressed in a protective asbestos suit and placed inside a house. He and the house were then set on fire. The suit was put on very carefully, for any gaps or holes in it could have resulted in Bud being severely burned, or even killed. Here Bud, himself on fire, runs from the burning house.

Right: Hal Needham, pictured directing the film *Smokey and the Bandit*, is also one of Hollywood's top stuntmen, with a number of stunting records to his credit.

a remarkable leap in a car across London's Tower Bridge as the arms were being raised.

"We did that stunt early one Sunday morning," he said. "Naturally, I'd worked everything out beforehand, down to the last detail. There were seven cameras to film it. I approached the bridge at about 70 mph, then up and over I went. I was airborne for 58 ft. When the car hit the other side there was a tremendous bump, the windscreen shattered and the car chassis bent in. The car was in a terrible mess, with steam pouring out. But I was OK and felt terrific."

Peter, who fell 65 feet from a helicopter in *Sky Riders*, and was set on fire for one minute 15 seconds in *Shout at the Devil*, once had a shock while doing a car stunt in the Oliver Reed film *Sitting Target*. After leaping over another car, the steering wheel of the car he was driving came off in his hand.

"The car ploughed straight into a wall," he said. "I was lucky to come out of that with just a few bruises and grazes."

It didn't put him off stunt work, though. "When you know you've done a great piece of work, then there's no other feeling like it in the world," he said.

One of Hollywood's top stunt men is Hal Needham. Hal once did an amazing stunt for an advertising commercial by driving a car (or rather, 'flying' a car) across a lake. He achieved it by putting a 15,000 horsepower rocket motor in the back of the car.

He reckons he has broken 42 bones, and has twice broken his back, but says he just couldn't give up the stunt business.

He holds a number of world records in stunting, one of which is for 'boat jumping', when he guided a craft 138 feet through the air in a swamp in Georgia for the Burt Reynolds film *Gator*.

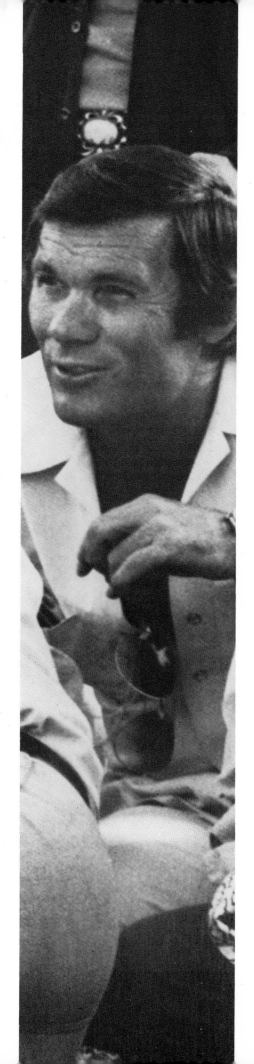

Screen Stuntmen
Star Stunts

In the early days of cinema, the stars would perform their own stunts. Stars of the silent screen, such as Harold Lloyd, would take enormous risks in order to amuse their audiences. But as the action grew more and more dangerous, the stuntman came into his own, and gradually the professional stuntmen took over most of the dangerous work.

Today, more stars are going back to performing at least some of the stunts themselves.

Clint Eastwood risked his neck by having himself lowered from a helicopter on to the top of a narrow

Left: James Garner (centre) himself performed many of the exciting car stunts in the film *Grand Prix.* Below: Steve McQueen (left) and Paul Newman appeared together in many dangerous sequences in the much-acclaimed film *The Towering Inferno.*

Stuntman—By Accident

One of the most surprised men in Hollywood recently was a painter at Universal Studios.

The studio has on show 'Bruce', the mechanical shark which starred in *Jaws.* Every afternoon the shark 'attacks' a fisherman in a rowing boat, rips away a pier and finally jumps ten feet out of the water.

The painter was touching up a worn spot on Bruce's fin when he accidentally activated the mechanism. The shark threw him in the air and then dragged him through the water.

Fortunately he survived— but he isn't thinking of taking up stunt work as a career!

Screen Stuntmen

Left and above: Clint Eastwood and crew risking their necks 600 feet up on top of a narrow pillar of rock during the filming of *The Eiger Sanction*. Right: Clint, one of several stars now performing some of their own stunts, in training for his rôle.

pillar of rock standing 600 feet above a valley floor for some very dangerous scenes in *The Eiger Sanction*. James Garner took many risks at the wheel of a racing car in *Grand Prix*. Paul Newman likes to do his own stunts where possible.

But the star who has perhaps taken the most risks is Steve McQueen. In fact, he was presented with a silver buckle by the Stuntmen's Association of Motion Pictures in America.

Among his more spectacular stunts were a motorcycle chase in *Getaway*, some spirited riding in Western films, and some of the motor racing scenes in *Bullitt*. In fact, he was so annoyed at the suggestion that he had not done the driving in *Bullitt* that he entered for a motor race at Sebring —and finished second.

Screen Stuntmen
James Bond Stunts

The James Bond films are famous for their spectacular stunt work, and one of the men behind many of these stunts is Bob Simmons.

For the first Bond film *Dr. No*, he let a live tarantula spider walk up his arm. In *Thunderball* he plunged into a shark-infested pool.

In the same film he also performed one of his most dangerous stunts when he drove a car which was blown up by a chasing motorcyclist firing rockets at him.

"We used real high explosives for that stunt," he said. He had a quarter-inch plate put into the back of the car seat for extra protection but the impact was so great that the car burst into flames and rolled off the road. Bob managed to fall clear, but members of the film unit had a worrying few minutes when they thought he was still in the car.

In *The Man With the Golden Gun* a car was seen to turn over completely in corkscrew fashion as it jumped across a river from one bank to the other (see left).

A computer was used to plan the stunt. Information was fed into the machine which then worked out the leap and even drew an animated cartoon of the catapulting car jumping 50 feet from one ramp to another, reaching a top height of 65 feet while spiralling 360 degrees in the air.

A special take-off ramp was constructed to meet the specification of the computer. At the wheel of the car was American Loren 'Bumps' Willert. When he revved off, an ambulance, a crane and two frogmen were standing by in case he came down in the river. But they were not required. 'Bumps' roared away on his 45 mph approach run, hit the ramp at the perfect angle, then up he went into his full mid-air roll and landed safely on the other side.

The stunt was all over in a few seconds, but the preparations for it had taken countless hours of meticulous planning.

Left: A thrilling 10-second sequence filmed near Bangkok for the James Bond epic, *The Man With the Golden Gun*. Top stuntman Loren Willert, standing in for star Roger Moore, 'flew' the car 50 feet across the river. His success earned him champagne and a 1,000 dollar bonus! The cost of the sequence? £120,000! Right: Stuntman Bob Heron crashes a car through a barn roof in a hair-raising episode from the film *Convoy*.

Screen Stuntmen

Above: A dramatic moment from the film *Hollywood Cowboy*. Right: Joe Bologna and Stockard Channing wait, apparently unconcerned, as their bus teeters on the

edge of a cliff in Old Tunjunja Canyon in California, during the filming of *The Big Bus*. Terror enters their faces as filming begins!

Risks for the Film Crew

In some films, it isn't only the stars and stunt artists who take risks. For instance, the recent film *The Deep* takes place mostly under water. In order to film it, the director, actors, actresses and camera crew had to learn to dive. They then had to work at the bottom of the sea at depths of up to 200 feet, for periods of between 40 minutes and an hour.

The stuntmen faced even greater problems: they had to wrestle with real sharks!

For the shooting of the film, each sequence was carefully planned beforehand, so as not to waste time once the film crew and the stars had dived, and a system of signals was prepared so that they could communicate with each other while under water.

DID YOU KNOW. . . ?

. . . that cars are sometimes put on casters for stunts, so that they'll spin more easily.

. . . that old Jaguars are ideal for smashes because they're easy to match if duplicates are needed. Sometimes six or ten cars are used before a sequence is right.

. . . that for safety in an impending car smash, the petrol tank is removed and a gravity-fed container substituted for the petrol pump, with just enough petrol to move the car a few yards.

40

Screen Stuntmen

Above: Stuntman A. J. Bakunas pictured during a spectacular 196-foot jump from a bridge spanning Hurricane Creek in Utah, staged for the film *The Car*. Bakunas died stunting on 23 September 1978. Above: Daredevil stuntwoman Janet Brady jumps a Pontiac over a fence and into a park for the film *Smokey and the Bandit*.

Marty Feldman, performing one of his own stunts for *The Last Remake of Beau Geste*—an irreverent version of P. C. Wren's classic tale about the French Foreign Legion.

. . . that stunt horse riders sometimes use stirrups without sides, to release their feet quickly.

. . . that riders have a carefully disguised sand pit to fall into when they fall at full gallop. So even if the ground *looks* hard, it isn't—providing they fall in the right place, of course!

. . . that a stunt pilot in *Aces High* flew home upside down to keep a wing in place after it had broken. As he came in to land he turned up the right way and did a belly flop landing, making a thirty-foot corkscrew groove in the grass!

Screen Stuntmen
Small Screen Stunts

Although the cinema screen shows many of the most spectacular achievements of the stuntmen, the smaller screen of television frequently portrays thrilling chases and dangerous exploits which are just as difficult. Sometimes, as in *The Sweeney, Bionic Woman* and *Six Million Dollar Man,* the stunts are in many ways similar to those on the big screen; others, such as those performed by Michael Crawford in the successful B.B.C. comedy series *Some Mothers Do 'Ave 'Em,* are essentially planned for the small television screen.

Michael chose to do all the stunt work himself. During the course of the series this involved him in hanging over cliffs, falling through floorboards, hanging from a workmen's cradle outside an office block and roller skating between the wheels of a moving juggernaut lorry.

All the stunts were carefully planned and prepared by the team of writer, producer and actors. Once they had decided on a stunt, the B.B.C.'s visual effects department would take over to plan exactly how to perform it. They practised with models until they were satisfied that the stunt was at least reasonably safe to do, but the actual equipment to be used was not normally set up until the day of shooting. Then three cameras would be positioned from different angles so that the stunt would only have to be performed once, but the editor would have a choice of shots.

Many of the stunts relied on the quick reactions and reliability of other people. For instance, when Michael Crawford roller skated underneath a huge lorry he had to rely on the driver's skill as well as his own. Although it was filmed with the lorry moving very slowly, and then speeded up on film afterwards, it was still a very dangerous thing to do. Even a slow-moving lorry could inflict considerable damage on a roller skater.

Most of the roller skating sequence was shot at top speed, even the part where he skated down steps and headed full tilt towards a concrete bollard, only parting his legs at the last moment to go past it.

One stunt which didn't go so well left him suspended from a workmen's cradle fifty feet in the air for over half an hour.

42

Screen Stuntmen

The plan had been for him to appear to fall from the cradle and hang from it, holding on to his workmate (a stuntman) by the hand. The filming should have taken only a few minutes and the men would have been brought to safety immediately. But the plan went wrong.

An assistant was lying unseen at the bottom of the cradle, which was intended for only two people. The extra weight caused the bottom of the cradle to jump out of its ramp. The whole thing swung sideways against the building, so that it could not be lowered to the ground. While the production team debated what to do, the stuntman and assistant were at least inside the cradle; Michael Crawford was hanging over the side. In fact, he still appeared to be clinging to the stuntman's hand, though of course he was tied with ropes which the cameras could not see.

It took over half an hour to inch the cradle slowly to the top of the building and bring them all to safety.

Fortunately that was the only stunt that went really wrong. But it takes a cool head and iron nerve to take this sort of risk.

Another star takes chances. Jean-Paul Belmondo, as Inspector le Tellier, makes dangerous progress in his pursuit of a mad killer in *The Night Callers*.

43

Screen Stuntmen
Stuntman in Focus

Vic Armstrong is a rugged, smiling thirty-two-year-old, who is already a veteran stuntman. He's been in the business for fourteen years and is still one of the youngest, as well as one of the most successful names, in film stunting. His versatility as an athlete is stunning—he's a specialist in riding, skin-diving, motor-cycling and free-fall stunts, and performs the most horrifying stunts with cars. In one sequence for the film *On Her Majesty's Secret Service,* no fewer than twelve Ford Escorts, one Mercedes, one Camaro and two Minis were written off.

Vic has doubled for stars like Gregory Peck, Malcolm McDowell, Robert Shaw, George Lazenby, Roger Moore, Simon Ward, Anthony Quinn, Richard Chamberlain and Michael York. He is greatly in demand and no sooner has he finished one film than he is off to film new sequences in locations all over the world.

There are many things to take into account when doubling for a star. Like him, the stuntman has to act, but he also has to keep his face hidden most of the time. He has to

wear padded clothing, and it is the job of the costume department to make sure the stuntman is well protected without being too bulky.

Stunting means work-outs to keep supple and fit, a three-mile run every day, playing squash, and an hour's ride each morning. Too much gymnasium work is bad—it increases your size too much. It means watching your diet, even on location in remote parts of the world, where you have to eat whatever food is available. On no account must the stuntman put on much weight, and look bigger than the star for whom he's standing in!

The stuntman has to risk his life with every stunt. Vic once broke a shinbone in Morocco and found himself in the local maternity hospital—the only sterile place in the area! He was in hospital for six days, was riding again within seven weeks and doing stunt riding falls within eleven weeks of his accident. There's no time to be lost when time is money. You need quick reflexes, an athletic build, nerves of steel and a lot of luck to survive in the stunt business. Vic has all these qualities, and a lot of talent besides.

Below: A stunt that misfired. Vic had to time his fall to the split second in order to crash on to a small section of breakable wooden posts. Unfortunately, he slightly mistimed the fall and landed, painfully, on some of the metal posts instead.

Below: *The Great Waldo Pepper* is a film about pilots from the First World War who became 'barnstormers' in the American Mid-West in the 1930s. 'Barnstormers' were acrobatic, daredevil fliers. While in flight some climbed out of the cockpits of their planes and on to the wings, others clambered up rope ladders from one plane to another. They flew down streets at roof-top level, through trees, under bridges and stormed through barns open at both ends (hence their name). They seldom wore parachutes and few had proper flying clothing!

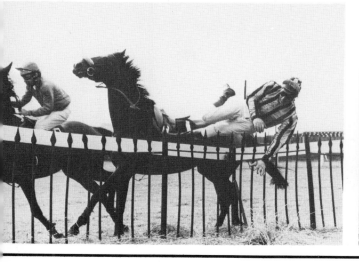

Against the Sea

One of the starters in the 1968 Transatlantic race was Lt. Leslie Williams R.N. in his 53-foot sloop-rigged *Spirit of Cutty Sark*. He was a highly experienced sailor, having skippered the Naval Sail Training Yacht *Merlin* in the 1964 Tall Ships Race, and competed in the Round Britain Race.

Clare Francis

One of the most intrepid lone sailors of recent years has been a woman—Clare Francis.

She had the most unlikely start for a sailor: after being educated at local schools in Surrey she joined the Royal Ballet School. From there she went on to take a degree in economics at University College, London.

But she tired of the sophistication of city life, bought a boat and decided to sail it to America with some friends. The friends all backed out one by one, and Clare was left to make the trip alone. It took her 37 days: three days less than the women's record.

After spending the winter in the West Indies, she sailed back to England to take part in the 2000 mile *Observer* Round Britain Race, coming third out of 61 entrants.

This caught the attention of Ron and Joan Green, who offered to lend her their new boat, an Ohlson 38, to take part in the 1976 Transatlantic Race. She entered the boat, now named *Robertson's Golly,* in the Azores Race, and qualified for the *Observer* Transatlantic.

On 5 June 1976, Clare was one of 125 contestants taking part in the race. It was a terrible crossing with storms and high winds for much of the way, but Clare battled on in the teeth of the gales. She sailed into Newport, Rhode Island, 29 days later with her self-steering gear broken, to take thirteenth place. She also created a new women's single-handed transatlantic record, for which she was awarded the Mary Thomas Trophy.

Her outstanding courage has since been recognised by a number of awards: the M.B.E. in the 1978 New Year Honours List; the Sir Max Aitken Award for outstanding bravery; and the magnificent 'Francis Chichester Trophy', which had only been awarded four times previously.

Right: Clare Francis, one of the most courageous of the lone yachtsmen, takes a well-earned rest and snack during one of her journeys. Below: Clare, this time minus her protective oilskins, and wearing a hat to protect her head from the strong ocean sun, checks that some of the vital equipment on her vessel is in order.

Against the Sea
The Observer
Single-Handed Race

The North Atlantic is a frightening place. Even at the height of summer, it is raked by storm-force winds, drifting icebergs and swirling fogs. So to sail a yacht from England to the United States is no easy undertaking, even if the boat is well-proven and the crew thoroughly experienced in ocean crossings.

But to set out across those 3000 perilous miles of sea single-handed, or to do it in a craft of revolutionary and unproven design, seems positively foolhardy. Yet the number of sailing enthusiasts who want to sail in the *Observer*-sponsored Single-Handed Transatlantic Race grows at an incredible pace. When the race was first run, in 1960, there were just five intrepid single-handers ready

to face up to the rigours of the North Atlantic. By 1976 the starting fleet had increased to 125 yachts of all shapes, sizes and sail-plans, from a 22½-foot overgrown dinghy to a gigantic 236-foot four-masted schooner.

Like the Olympics, the race takes place every four years. In the five races run since 1960, no fewer than 245 single-handed yachts have sailed out of Plymouth Sound and set course for America. Of these, 151 reached the target ports of New York or Newport, Rhode Island within the time limits of the race. A few have straggled in later, but more than 80 boats and skippers had to retire from the race.

Some of the retirements were straightforward—steering gear failure that made it more sensible

for a vessel to turn back, or a broken battery that prevented the skipper from showing proper navigation lights at night. But each race has had its share of intense drama too.

In 1960 the race began from Plymouth with the minimum of public interest. There were just five boats entered and about the same number of spectator craft drew out of Plymouth to wave them away.

A little-known map publisher named Francis Chichester was the favourite in the bookies' list (he did win comfortably, 40 days later), but there were also eyes for Dr. David Lewis, a New Zealander by adoption, who was at the helm of a 25-foot sloop called *Cardinal Vertue*.

Left: Sandy Munro, an ex-Fleet Air Arm pilot, aboard his 45-foot catamaran *Ocean Highlander*, which lies deep in the trough of an Atlantic wave. Above: Brian Cooke, a bank manager when ashore, hoists the mainsail of his 32-foot sloop *Opus*. Continual altering of the sails to make the best of varying wind conditions is one of the lone yachtsman's most exhausting tasks while at sea.

The race finished that year in New York and the most direct route was along the Great Circle, looping across the ocean so as to pass close to Newfoundland and Nova Scotia before running down the eastern seaboard of the States. Lewis kept strictly to that path, although it meant sailing hard into the prevailing south-westerlies and Atlantic currents. For the first two-thirds of the voyage things went reasonably well; then his troubles began.

First he was sighted by a Canadian frigate. A tiny yacht in those vast expanses of ocean is a very rare sight indeed, and the Canadians were understandably anxious to find out if Lewis was fit and well. They came closer and closer, blanketing out whatever wind there was for the 25-footer, until her skipper was quite unable to control her movements. Crash! *Cardinal Vertue*'s mast smashed against the steel hull of the frigate and the lower port spreader collapsed. Luckily the mast did not come down but the shame-faced Canadians soon pulled away and left Lewis to make his repairs in peace.

Then the weather forced him much further west than he had meant to go before turning down the coast. This meant he had to pass inside the notorious Sable Island—graveyard of many ships—and down the coast of Nova Scotia in thick fog. That was frightening enough, but worse was to come. Lewis realised that he was so far inland, and there was such an unfavourable wind, that he would have terrible difficulty clawing back out to sea in order to round Martha's Vineyard and Nantucket Island. He decided to take the chance of sailing through Pollock Rip, a narrow stretch of water between Martha's Vineyard and the coast which is justly feared for its ferocious tides and treacherous shallows.

After he had decided to take the risk, the fog came down and he worked out that he would have to tackle the worst part of the passage in the middle of the night!

Imagine trying to steer a small yacht through a narrow channel in

Against the Sea

flukey winds, at night, with a ripping tide fighting you every inch of the way, and fog all around. Then to hear, as Lewis did, the sound of surf breaking on rocks somewhere nearby. But where? He had no choice but to sail on, waiting every second for the ominous thud of keel on rock which would signal that the yacht had run aground, maybe to hold fast until she had smashed herself to pieces.

In fact, *Cardinal Vertue* did touch bottom once, but Lewis was able to get her clear again and at last he emerged into open water and the prospect of a clear sail down to New York and the finishing line. He crossed it 56 days after leaving Plymouth, shaken and weary. But he was ready to go again in 1964.

That year saw the first triumph of the French in the *Observer* Single-Handed. A young, stocky Breton called Eric Tabarly, a lieutenant in the French Navy, romped home first (to Newport, Rhode Island) in just over 27 days. That was six days faster than the previous record set by Francis Chichester, and it seemed that he must have enjoyed a fast and trouble-free sail.

Not at all. In fact, Tabarly had lost the single-hander's most valuable aid, his self-steering gear, just a week after the start. He lost the blade of the gear only a few days out and pulled the whole mechanism inboard to repair it, only to find that a sheared bolt would not budge and the gear was useless. Now, self-steering is absolutely

vital to the solo sailor. It allows the boat to sail herself so that he can change sails, navigate, write up his log, eat and rest. Without it all these tasks have to be snatched in the rare moments when the wind is light enough—and steady enough —for the sail-plan to be balanced so that the yacht will sail steadily with the tiller lashed.

From the end of that first week of the race, Tabarly was fighting a constant battle with the boat and with his own fatigue. He could not sleep for more than 90 minutes at a time at any stage of the voyage and for two whole days before he crossed the finishing line he did not sleep at all.

All this was made more complicated by the fact that he found his log was not functioning properly,

Against the Sea

so it was difficult to tell how far the boat had travelled, and thus to make accurate navigation fixes. And his alarm clock gave up the ghost. Imagine trying to shake yourself into wakefulness every hour or so, without the help of even an alarm clock. The Frenchman was tempted at first to stop racing and simply cruise easily across the ocean. "But then I thought what a figure I should cut when I got back to France and told my tale of woe to all those who had helped me and encouraged me. The least I could do was try to finish the race."

And finish he did, nearly three days ahead of anybody else. But not before another drama. A block at the mast head worked loose and the skipper was forced to haul himself aloft in a bosun's chair to

In the 1976 single-handed Transatlantic race, the boat which attracted the most publicity was the four-masted French schooner, *Club Mediterranée*. Sailed by Alain Colas, the winner of the previous race in 1972, and measuring 236 feet in length, the vessel was easily the largest of all the boats taking part that year. A record entry of 125 vessels set out from Plymouth Sound, and the huge four-master is pictured here at the start of the race, under full sail, with the French tricolour fluttering from her stern.

repair it. It took him three attempts and a whole morning's work, but eventually it was done.

Wracked with fatigue as he was, Tabarly had forced his aching limbs to hoist his own weight three times up that mast and then to cling on desperately as the mast gyrated wildly from side to side.

Little wonder that Tabarly became an overnight hero in France and General de Gaulle instantly made him a Chevalier of the Legion of Honour.

The bad weather of 1968 forced 19 retirements from the *Observer* Single-Handed out of the fleet of 35 starters, and it was Britain's Geoffrey Williams who finally won. But the French took over in 1972 when Alain Colas sailed the big trimaran *Pen Duick IV* into Newport ahead

Against the Sea

of the pack after a much quieter and faster run.

But Colas did not get all the headlines. Most of the British papers devoted more space to that map publisher who had won the first *Observer* Single-Handed race, the world-renowned solo sailor Sir Francis Chichester. Though he looked tired and ill, Sir Francis sailed off in *Gipsy Moth V* that June, hoping to match or beat his earlier crossings.

It was not to be. Within a week he had decided to return to Plymouth, weary after a fierce gale and fatigued even further by coping with a broken control wire on his self-steering gear. He failed to make the scheduled broadcasts to the *Sunday Times* and fears began to grow that the frail old sailor was in serious danger. An RAF Nimrod located him 600 miles south-west of Land's End, but flew by so fast that he could only flash the message "tired and weak" to them to explain why he was giving up.

The HMS *Salisbury*, a naval frigate, was detailed to find *Gipsy Moth*, and Sir Francis's son Giles was flown out to the ship.

Meanwhile the French weather ship *France II* had steamed to *Gipsy Moth* to offer assistance. Several times Sir Francis signalled the message "I am O.K." and was relieved to see the weather men pulling back the rubber dinghy they had been preparing to launch.

Later he heard a hoot, and found the *France II* almost alongside his small dinghy and a man on the bridge asking where he was heading. He shouted "Plymouth" and hoped they would go away, but the ship stayed with him until it was not possible to avoid a collision. The crosstrees of *Gipsy Moth*'s mizzen mast caught in the ship's portholes and the shrouds were snapped, while the top of the mast bent crazily. Later it snapped and ripped the mizzen sail.

Later the *Salisbury* found *Gipsy Moth* and transferred Giles Chichester and some riggers

aboard to effect repairs.

One of the casualties of the 1976 race was Pierre Fehlmann, a Swiss who had seemed a likely winner of the intermediate size yacht class. His long, slim yacht *Gauloises* was clearly light and fast, but proved unable to withstand the terrible pounding of the Atlantic storms that year.

Nine days after the start, Land's End radio station heard from the weather ship *Romeo* that *Gauloises* was leaking badly and the skipper needed urgent assistance. Portishead radio alerted all shipping in the area and *Atlantic Conveyor* was first to find Fehlmann. The problems of saving a lone yachtsman with a cliff-sided monster freighter are best told in Captain O'Brien's own words.

"I have never seen such a ter-

Sir Francis Chichester set out in 1972 to try to better his earlier Atlantic crossings. Concern for him mounted when he failed to make four scheduled radio calls. An RAF Nimrod located him about 200 miles off the French coast, and picked up his message —"tired and weak". The picture above shows Sir Francis (arrowed) on board *Gipsy Moth V*, as seen by the Nimrod, already on his way back to England.

rifying prospect in all my 47 years at sea," he said later. "The weather was very bad with a storm of wind force 9 or 10. We were plugging straight into the teeth of it, and there was certainly no possibility of putting a boat into the water.

"We got gangway nets and safety harnesses and suspended them over the starboard side of the ship. Then Fehlmann behaved in a very intelligent way. He is certainly a courageous sailor."

In fact, Fehlmann had little option. By now his yacht was sinking fast and her mast had come down. It was a choice between a last gasp leap for the huge conveyor ship or certain death in the gigantic breakers of those storm-tossed seas. The *Atlantic Conveyor* came as close to the yacht as the master dared at about three in the morning.

"He used the hull of the yacht as a sail in that terrific wind and managed to steer *Gauloises* alongside. Although we put some oil over the side to calm the water we knew he would not be able to swim, so he had to get it right first time. He managed to bring his boat close enough to be able to jump across into the netting. The boat heeled and he was pushed under the water, but he hung on and managed to clamber up the netting and into the boat. He got away with his wet suit and his passport—and that's about all."

Fehlmann was lucky. Luckier than some who have taken part in the race. Two skippers of the 125 who set sail in 1976 were never seen again. Yet the clamour for places in the 1980 fleet is already growing. The single-handed sailor is a special kind of dangerman —the loner who wants to prove his strength, skill and seamanship against one of the most daunting ocean passages in the world. Those who have succeeded in reaching America can feel proud. To win a trophy is great: but simply to have crossed that ocean single-handed is a triumph.

Rowing Across the Oceans

Setting out to sail the Atlantic Ocean is a formidable task, but at least the yachtsman has the power of the wind to help him on his way. The oarsman has nothing but his own muscle to pull his boat across the waves in the teeth of the storms and heavy seas which he can meet there.

But this has not deterred a number of people from pitting their strength in rowing boats against the might of the oceans.

Among the first to try were Captain John Ridgway and Sergeant Charles Blyth. They set out in *English Rose III* to row the 3000 miles across the Atlantic in 1966.

Above: John Ridgway and Charles Blyth in *English Rose III*, during their successful attempt to row the Atlantic. Right: Lone oarsman Tom (Moby) McClean gives a victory salute from his boat *Super Silver*. He beat Ridgway and Blyth's record by a staggering 20 days.

They succeeded in making the crossing in 92 days.

This record was beaten less than three years later by Tom McClean, a paratrooper from the same regiment as Ridgway and Blyth. McClean set out with no advance publicity, and said afterwards that he only made the attempt because somebody bet him five shillings that he could not row the Atlantic single-handed.

Living on meat cubes, sardines, cheese, biscuits and vitamin pills, McClean emerged from the sea on the Irish coast only 72 days after setting out from Newfoundland.

Later he admitted that his only previous rowing experience was on a boating pool. He made his epic crossing in a 20-foot boat, *Super Silver*, armed only with "A Beginner's Guide to the Sea" and two books on navigation.

Against the Sea
Alone Around the World

The first man known to have sailed right round the world was Sir Francis Drake. But he took three years, and his crew numbered about 35 people.

The first man recorded as having sailed around the world all alone was Captain Joshua Slocum who made the voyage in 1895. Like Sir Francis Drake, he took about three years.

It was not until 1967 that the round-the-world trip was made single-handed and quickly. Then it was done by that intrepid sailor Sir Francis Chichester (then Mr Francis Chichester).

He did not have an easy time. He was 64 years old when he set out and had been ill with cancer. He set off with an injured leg, and among the problems he had to face on the long journey to Australia were trouble with the self-steering gear and constant battles with the weather, including a sudden squall which threatened to turn the boat right over.

However, he reached Sydney safely after just 107 days, and spent seven weeks there effecting necessary repairs to the boat.

By the time he reached Australia he had used up most of his reserves of strength. But he refused to listen to friends who urged him to give up. They knew he had to face the might of the Tasman Sea on the return trip—six thousand miles of difficult sailing through the Roaring Forties and the Shrieking Fifties, and after that Cape Horn!

"No matter what anyone says," Chichester announced, "I am going to set sail."

So *Gipsy Moth IV* went back to sea to face the fearful return trip.

She was storm-battered almost from the first minute. After only two days at sea, he woke to find his

Against the Sea

belongings cascading round him. The yacht had been hit by a freak wave and completely overturned so that its mast was below the surface of the water. The lockers had come open and plates, knives, tins and other goods were falling out.

Fortunately she gradually righted herself, and Chichester was able to see how much damage had been done: the floor was deep in water and food, tools and other equipment were swimming around in it. The forehatch had come open and water was pouring in, so he had to fight to get that closed first of all, otherwise the vessel would have sunk.

Apart from that, he was fortunate in having suffered no real damage and he was able to go on with his voyage. But some valuable equipment had been swept over the side, including a sail and several hundred feet of line.

The journey round the Horn was difficult, and then he had to face again the Roaring Forties (latitudes 40° to 50°), notorious for their treacherous seas. But the small boat, though tossed by huge waves and battered by unfriendly seas, survived the worst that the elements could throw at her.

Chichester returned to England on 28 May 1967, to a welcome from hundreds of small craft and a ten-gun salute from the Royal Marines.

He had taken just nine months. In July he was knighted by the Queen, using the same sword as had been used to knight Sir Francis Drake.

By 1968 several people had sailed single-handed around the world, but they had all made at least one stop.

One of the results of the public interest aroused by the efforts of Sir Francis Chichester and later by Sir Alec Rose was that the *Sunday Times* decided to offer a prize for the fastest *non-stop* voyage around the world.

There were four contestants. One of them, Robin Knox-

Left: In 1967 Sir Francis Chichester (then plain Mr!) became the first man to sail single-handed around the world. His journey was made in *Gipsy Moth IV*, and he was knighted by the Queen on his return. He is pictured here in *Gipsy Moth V*. Above: Robin Knox-Johnston sits amongst the mounds of provisions he assembled for his epic, non-stop voyage around the world in 1968.

Johnston, was a former Merchant Navy officer, with considerable experience of the oceans of the world. His 32-foot ketch *Suhaili* had been built in India, and he had sailed it home to England via South Africa, so he was not new to long distance sailing, though he had not been alone on that journey.

He set off on 14 June 1968. Minor injuries such as a badly cut finger and small acid burns during the early stages did not deter him, and his little ketch battled bravely on in the face of heavy seas and appalling weather conditions.

Disaster struck with the failure of his self-steering gear. This meant that he could not set the boat on a course while he changed sails or snatched some much-needed sleep.

In despair, he considered giving up the attempt at Melbourne and satisfying himself with being the third person to sail non-stop from England to Australia.

But he managed to work out a means of balancing the sails so that the boat would stay on course, though at reduced speed, and this enabled him to get some sleep. Heartened by this success he began to feel that he could face up to the rest of the trip, and decided to continue his journey.

Not long after leaving Australia he again encountered storms and winds that would have deterred a less determined sailor, but by then he had heard the cheering news on his radio that he was believed to be in the lead and that one competitor in the race had given up.

After that, nothing would make him abandon the race.

More frustrations awaited him as he neared home. Just outside Falmouth he had to battle against head winds which forced him to take four days to cover just a few miles.

He finally landed at Falmouth, the first man ever to sail alone the whole way round the world without stopping.

It took him just 312 days, and among the official party to welcome him home was round-the-world sailor Sir Francis Chichester.

The Rescuers

Air/Sea Rescue

Bringing a helicopter down to hover close to the deck of a ship is a dangerous and highly skilled operation even in broad daylight and in good conditions.

To attempt it at night, when the pilot cannot see and the helicopter could get tangled up in the ship's masts and wires, makes the task still more difficult.

Add to that the fact that emergencies nearly always happen in the worst weather, and you have some idea of what the men of helicopter air/sea rescue face.

Typical of their rescues was the night in 1974 when the Polish trawler *Nurzec* ran aground off Murcar near Aberdeen in a Force 10 gale. A lifeboat from the Russian tug *Gordiy* took some men off the trawler but capsized on its way back.

At that point, British Airways helicopter air/sea rescue service was called in. In pitch darkness, and in the teeth of a howling gale, they located the men in the sea and brought them to safety. They then returned to the *Nurzec* and faced the appallingly difficult task of holding the helicopter steady enough to winch the men up from the trawler. Despite the gale and the darkness, four men were safely winched up that night. The remaining four were taken off the following morning.

But it was a daytime rescue which won for the men of British Airways air/sea rescue the award of the Coastguard "Rescue Shield" for 1973/4.

It was awarded to them after a particularly heroic rescue. The British trawler *Navena* had foundered on rocks near Copinsay Island in the Orkneys, and it looked as though the ship would break up.

The howling winds were north-erly gale Force 10 with hail squalls. When the helicopter arrived the ship's crew were sheltering by the wheelhouse amidships, and the deck was being swept by huge waves. For each rescue, the winchman was lowered to the deck; a crew member ran from the wheelhouse to the winchman who secured a lifting strop around him so that they could both

A seaman being rescued from the British ship *Lady Jean*. A close look at the picture shows that it is a 'double lift' with the winchman going down to the deck to take the seaman off. There was a Force 10 gale at the time which made the ship buck and toss and buffeted the helicopter, nearly blowing it away from the ship. But despite the near-impossible conditions, ten men were successfully rescued.

The Rescuers

be lifted back into the helicopter. The two winchmen on that rescue, Terry Chappell and Ted Clarke, each made six trips down to the deck and back again.

Despite the appalling conditions, the helicopter took only 35 minutes to save the lives of twelve men.

The men of air/sea rescue are called out to many types of emergency. Some jobs are routine to them, though of vital importance to those they rescue. For instance, they are often called to lift off seamen who have been taken ill or had an accident. On these occasions a doctor often flies with them to give immediate treatment. Each rescue helicopter carries a range of medical equipment.

Another task for them is to lift off the entire crew of oil rigs when the weather is too bad for them to stay safely on the rig. Where possible, this is carried out before the weather gets too bad, as the oil

companies prefer to lift their men to safety before conditions become dangerous. But when bad weather strikes suddenly, the oil men can find themselves in considerable danger, with their lives depending on the helicopter men.

The air/sea rescue service is provided on a 24-hour basis. At Aberdeen, the men of British Airways helicopters air/sea rescue service maintain a round-the-clock alert for emergencies, whilst in Norfolk it is the men of RAF Coltishall who are always ready to help ships caught by the strong winds and high seas of the East Coast.

Whichever helicopter service it is that provides the rescue, they often work in co-operation with other people, such as coastguards, lifeboat crews and the inshore rescue craft.

Why do they do it? The answer is provided by Terry Chappell, Rescue and Survival Officer for British Airways Helicopters at Aberdeen, who said, "We do this job because we get satisfaction out of providing a service which saves lives."

Top left: Royal Navy helicopters are active in rescues at sea. Here a helicopter crew is pictured taking part in a rescue from a stranded submarine. Above: The RAF, too, have helicopter teams skilled in air/sea rescue. Far left: May 1975: A rescue by British Airways helicopter air/sea rescue service. Crewman Pete Garland lands on the deck of the fishing vessel *Star of Peace* from the waiting helicopter to lift off a fisherman with a crushed hand. Left: Garland makes the 'Ready' signal to his colleagues, Gregson and Hill, in the helicopter. The rescue helicopters carry four crew—two pilots and two crewmen. Terry Chappell was the fourth member of the crew in this rescue.

The Rescuers

Teamwork

It takes teamwork to bring about a successful air/sea rescue. First, there is the four-man crew of the helicopter. This consists of two pilots: one to act as Captain and take the controls, and another to monitor the instruments and navigate; and there are two crewmen: a Winchman who goes down on the cable and a Winch Operator who guides the helicopter over the ship and operates the winch. Where more than one person is to be winched up, these two usually take it in turns to go down on the cable. On occasions, a doctor also travels with the crew.

But these people would be of no use without the back-up team at the base.

There are the engineers who maintain the helicopters to a high standard of readiness so that they can take off within minutes of a distress call being received. And there are the operations staff who maintain the vital link between the traffic control rescue centre, the helicopter and the vessel; and who co-ordinate the movements of pilots, engineers and rescue crewmen.

Teamwork: the essence of a successful rescue.

Above: A Royal Navy helicopter takes part in the rescue of a casualty, who has been lifted off the treacherous rocks below. People who are injured or seriously ill will be firmly strapped to a stretcher, as shown in the picture, and winched up to the waiting helicopter. Far right: A crewman assists a man to the waiting Royal Navy helicopter by means of a rescue strop (see right). In difficult rescue conditions helicopters may work in conjunction with other services. The RAF may call out aircraft, as well as its own helicopters. The aircraft are often very useful in locating the scene of a rescue and directing helicopters to it. Right: The winchman and navigator of an RAF search and rescue helicopter stand by to take part in a rescue.

The Rescuers

THE SINGLE LIFT PROCEDURE

If you should have the misfortune to need to be rescued by helicopter, you will be lifted in a rescue strop. This is what it looks like.

In most cases a helicopter crewman will be lowered to you and he will put the strop on. Do as you are told and nothing else. If no crewman is winched down but the strop is lowered on its own this is how to put it on:

1 Grasp the strop and put both arms and your head through the loop.

2 Make sure that the wide padded part is as high as possible across the back, with the two straps coming under your armpits and up in front of your face.

3 Pull the toggle down as far as possible.

4 When you are ready to be lifted, look up at the helicopter, put one arm out to full extent and give a 'thumbs up'.

5 As you are lifted clear of the deck or water, make sure that your feet are not entangled in any ropes etc, then put both arms down by your sides.

6 As you are winched up alongside the helicopter *DO NOTHING.* You will be turned round so that you are facing away from the helicopter and pulled in so that you are sitting on the floor. You will then be told where to sit and the strop will be taken from you.

The Rescuers

Courage of a Lifeboatman

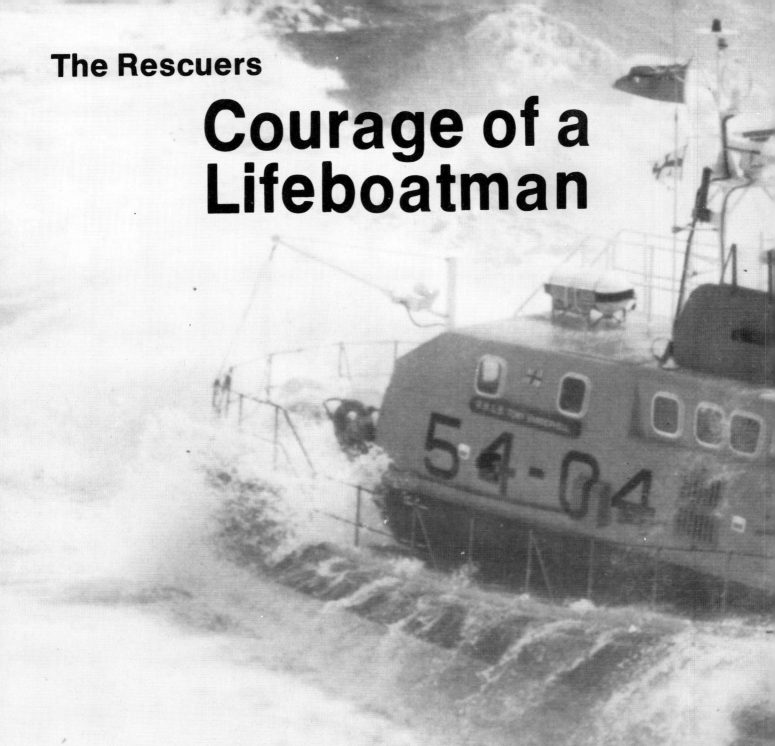

Battling up the East Coast in the teeth of a fierce gale blowing from the north east, the little Greek steamer *Pyrin* was in desperate straits. She was tossed about like a cork as giant waves thundered against her flimsy sides and swept in torrents across the deck and over the bridge.

The captain was a realist. He knew there was just one chance of safety for his ship and his crew. Cromer lay somewhere out there in the darkness off the port bow; if his ship could reach Cromer, it would be able to ride out the storm safely.

It was not to be. Just after eleven in the morning, the captain ordered a distress signal to be sent out. It was seen on shore and the Cromer lifeboat was ordered out.

But this was 1917. Most of the young fishermen were serving in the First World War or in the Merchant Navy. Those left behind were older men, some in their seventies. And the lifeboat was only a glorified rowing boat with sails, which had to be manhandled into the sea.

It took scores of men, straining and sweating, to get the lifeboat off the beach and into the mountainous breakers.

Then it took the 17-man crew nearly three hours to row two miles. For every move forward the waves would ensure a move back— like a grim game of snakes and

The Rescuers

The Rescuers

ladders. But they struggled on, until they reached the *Pyrin*, rescuing the crew of 16 men.

As they sipped mugs of hot cocoa and changed into dry clothes a message came: the Swedish ship, *Fernebo*, was in difficulties four miles off Cromer.

The men of Cromer were only human. They were old and they were wet and tired. Let some other lifeboat go. But no other lifeboat could be launched in the appalling conditions. Only the men of Cromer could rescue the Swedish sailors.

Coxswain Henry Blogg rallied his men, and they set out to face the seas again.

But their attempts to launch the lifeboat ended in failure; each time they tried, it was thrown back on to the shore.

On board the *Fernebo*, which had been blown in half by a mine, some of the crew saw this and decided to try to save themselves. Six of them launched a boat and rowed desperately for the shore. But fifty yards from safety the little boat capsized.

By now this had become a personal battle for the citizens of Cromer. A dozen bystanders linked hands and, chest-high in the surf, dragged the six men to safety.

The two halves of the ship were now driven ashore. The remainder of the crew were on the portion which stuck on a groyne, only 400 feet from safety. Several attempts were made to fire a line aboard to rescue them by breeches buoy, but they failed.

Blogg decided to try again to launch the lifeboat. This time they did get the boat into the water, but it was nearly smashed to pieces against the groyne and they were forced back to shore.

Then Blogg, one of the greatest lifeboatmen of all time, had an

Above: A dramatic aerial photograph shows the lifeboat from Cadgwith, on the Lizard peninsula in Cornwall, creating a mass of foaming white spray, as it shoots from the slipway on its way to answer a distress call at sea. Modern lifeboats are equipped with every kind of modern device—radio, radar and so on—so that their vital task may be carried out as quickly and effectively as possible.

inspiration: he saw a certain formation in the waves and reasoned that if he could get the lifeboat outside and above the Swedish boat, the waves might bring them alongside the wreck without smashing the boat to pieces against the groyne.

His strategy worked, and all the crew were saved.

During the time that Henry Blogg was coxswain of the Cromer lifeboat, he and his crew saved 873 lives. To honour him, a statue showing him clad in oilskins was erected on the cliff path at Cromer.

Mountain Rescue Teams at Work

The mist swirls around the mountain tops. Darkness closes in rapidly as night falls. And somewhere out there on the mountains, a group of climbers is lost.

Nobody knows what has happened to them. Have they lost their way? Are they huddled, cold and miserable, waiting to be found? Has somebody had a fall? All sorts of dangers spring to the minds of the people waiting for the climbers to return.

It is in situations like this that the Mountain Rescue Teams are called in.

These teams, consisting of highly experienced climbers who

know the area well, will turn out at short notice when people are in difficulties on the mountains.

Unpaid and having to provide their own equipment, the rescuers often face extremely hazardous situations in their attempts to save fellow human beings from danger.

Where a group of climbers has been lost, the first task facing the rescue team is to build up as complete a picture as possible. Where were the party heading for? How experienced were they? What equipment did they take? Any medical history? Weather conditions? Where were they last seen?

Once this has been done, a small group sets out to search all the likely tracks and paths. Missing parties are nearly always reported at night, when they fail to return to their base, so the dangers of searching for them are only too apparent: the darkness can be treacherous even for someone who knows the mountains well. In pitch blackness they pick their way care-

Dogs at Work

Dogs are often used to help in mountain rescues. They are sent out in the early stages of a search, before the scent has been destroyed. They follow mainly the ground scent of the lost people, but where people have been involved in a landslip or a fall, the dogs can still often trace them using the airborne scent of the air breathed out.

Left: An injured climber receives on-the-spot first aid from a member of Woodhead Mountain Rescue Team, before being transported to safety by stretcher (see pages 66 and 67).

Below: Mountain rescue teams, consisting of experienced climbers who know their particular area well, often have to undertake rescues in bad weather. Amid dense mist, which is making visibility difficult, a team prepares for a rescue bid.

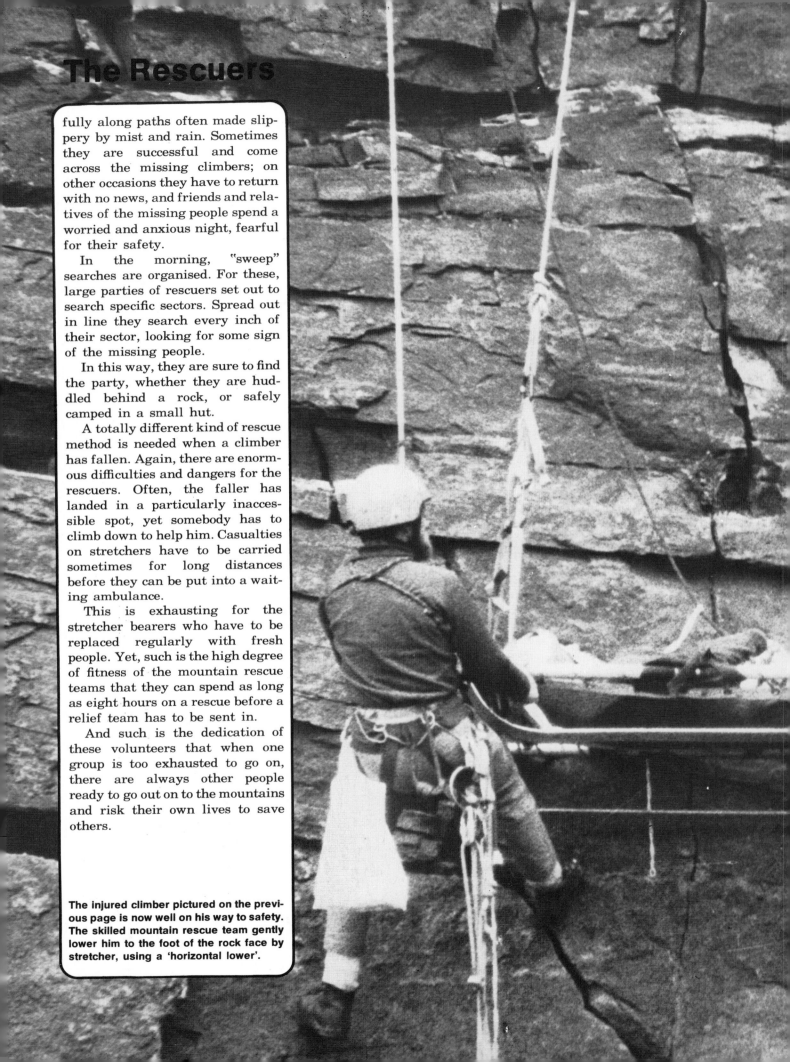

The Rescuers

fully along paths often made slippery by mist and rain. Sometimes they are successful and come across the missing climbers; on other occasions they have to return with no news, and friends and relatives of the missing people spend a worried and anxious night, fearful for their safety.

In the morning, "sweep" searches are organised. For these, large parties of rescuers set out to search specific sectors. Spread out in line they search every inch of their sector, looking for some sign of the missing people.

In this way, they are sure to find the party, whether they are huddled behind a rock, or safely camped in a small hut.

A totally different kind of rescue method is needed when a climber has fallen. Again, there are enormous difficulties and dangers for the rescuers. Often, the faller has landed in a particularly inaccessible spot, yet somebody has to climb down to help him. Casualties on stretchers have to be carried sometimes for long distances before they can be put into a waiting ambulance.

This is exhausting for the stretcher bearers who have to be replaced regularly with fresh people. Yet, such is the high degree of fitness of the mountain rescue teams that they can spend as long as eight hours on a rescue before a relief team has to be sent in.

And such is the dedication of these volunteers that when one group is too exhausted to go on, there are always other people ready to go out on to the mountains and risk their own lives to save others.

The injured climber pictured on the previous page is now well on his way to safety. The skilled mountain rescue team gently lower him to the foot of the rock face by stretcher, using a 'horizontal lower'.

The Rescuers

The Mountaineering Challenge

The Mountaineering Challenge
Then and Now

In the 19th century, mountaineering equipment usually consisted of little more than a few ropes, an axe or two and alpenstocks (spikes on poles which were often more of a hindrance than a help).

Mountaineers were often ill-prepared, and Lucy Walker, the first girl to climb the Matterhorn, did so wearing an ordinary print dress!

In those days, climbers generally followed the natural line of the mountain. That is to say, they followed the most obvious route up the mountain where there were hand and toe holds, outcrops of rock to hang on to, gullies to make progress easier and natural platforms on which to take a breather.

But by the 20th century, many of the exciting peaks had been conquered by the natural route. Climbers, eager for a challenge, began to look at artificial routes, that is, routes which took the most direct route up a mountain. For this reason, all sorts of equipment and devices were invented to help them. Often they would be confronted with a blank wall of rock with no holds whatsoever, and they would have to make use of expansion bolts, pitons and fixed ropes to get across.

The style of the game has changed; the name of the game remains: DANGER.

Left: Clouds ominously begin to gather behind the west shoulder of Mount Everest, the highest mountain in the world, and one whose challenge has attracted climbers again and again. To the right of Everest is Mount Nuptse. Right: Mountaineering has benefited greatly from the enormous range of modern equipment and clothing now available. This picture was taken in 1947!

The Mountaineering Challenge
A Himalayan Trilogy

A journey to the roof of the world—that was how one group of people celebrated the Queen's Jubilee in 1977.

Everest had been conquered in Coronation year, so it was fitting that the Jubilee should be celebrated by a return to the magnificent peaks of the Himalayas.

The 1977 North of England Himalayan Expedition, led by Paul Bean, had as its patron Major Cecil Crosthwaite, H.M. Lord Lieutenant of Cleveland County.

The group of seven mountaineers set off for the East Kulu Himalayas with two objectives: to climb the previously unconquered Point 20,300 and to climb White Sail by a new route.

Point 20,300, known only by its surveyed height, had caused much interest since it was first closely studied in 1965, but an expedition in 1976 failed to reach the summit. The North of England Expedition set out to face that challenge.

White Sail, at 21,148 feet, was the second highest peak of the area with ridges forming a connection with Papsura—the highest at 21,165 feet, and then Point 20,300. They all rise steeply from the heavily crevassed Papsura glacier to present a beautiful and impressive Himalayan Trilogy.

Paul Bean took an advance party to India on 4 May and established a temporary base camp at 12,000 feet. The rest of the party joined them a few days later and helped to establish the permanent base camp, and an advance base camp at 16,000 feet. This was done by 23 May.

On 25 May two groups set off from the advance camp. Rowland Perriment, Steve Berry and George Crawford-Smith were to try a direct route up White Sail, while Paul Bean, Barry Needle and Tara Chand set out to conquer the previously unclimbed Point 20,300.

The first day on Point 20,300 was difficult. Direct access to the route they hoped to take was barred by an ice fall, and the shortest way was threatened by avalanches. They decided to climb up on to a steep ridge that forms the end of the glacier.

Paul Bean wrote afterwards, "The steep climb is killing and once on the ridge at 11am the sun seems more determined than ever to destroy us. With heavy rucksacks and 12 inches of soft top surface each step takes a determined effort, but at least we've gained most of the height to our intended assault camp and the view over towards the mountainous border districts of Lahaul and Spitti with Tibet beyond, is a fascinating sight."

The three climbers set off again at 5.45am despite almost continuous lightning flashes and large anvil-shaped thunder clouds. Thick, powdery snow on top of the ice makes progress difficult, but the bad weather brings a sense of urgency to their climb.

"The previous day's climb to the site of the assault camp, the mental uncertainty of whether to ignore the approaching storm, the bad snow conditions and then finally the altitude have left me more shattered than I can ever remember. Barry (Barry Needle) is worse, but somehow keeps going. His first expedition to the Himalayas—and all that shows on his face is agony.

". . . My strength runs out at a final steep section just below the summit. I sink on to my knees and suck at the snow for moisture.

". . . Tara takes the lead. Rock hard water ice under soft snow . . . crampons clog up becoming useless weights attached to aching legs.

"Tara stops. 30 feet above him the snow meets a deep blue sky. We move up till there's no more up to go."

That was how Paul Bean described their moment of triumph as they stood on top of a previously unclimbed mountain. For Barry Needle it was a moment of mixed feelings: "I felt no elation, just

Above: The harsh, clear light of the Himalayan ranges adds dramatic effect to the silhouetted figures outlined against the sun. Here members of the expedition are routefinding on Papsura glacier.

Left: The advance base camp at Point 20,300, which the expedition renamed 'Devachen'—'the paradise of boundless light'. The south-west ridge of Papsura can be seen in the top right of the picture.

absolute and utter fatigue."

After just one hour the group set out on the downward descent, to be greeted at the camp by the disheartening news that the other expedition had failed in its attempt to climb White Sail.

Two of them, Rowland Merriment and George Crawford-Smith, decide to try again the next day.

Rowland describes the start: "All too soon it's 4.00am and I'm giving George a shake as I emerge into the pre-dawn freezing temperatures. The primus is coaxed into life with rapidly numbing fingers. Icicles provide our only water supply and breakfast of tea and porridge seems to take hours."

They set out in grey, cold weather and difficult climbing conditions. By 8.30am they have ascended 2,500 feet above the advance base and are just completing the steepest part of the snowfield.

They have climbed above the cloud but are aware that the sun will cause the snow conditions to deteriorate rapidly.

Rowland writes: "The air is getting noticeably thinner and the snow softer. Each step is taking more effort and the cloud layer has moved up to envelop us. The mountains take on a more sinister atmosphere. Still we plod on with gaps between rests decreasing and instead of ice axes used for support, a rest is usually an uncontrolled collapse into the snow. At the end of each 150-foot pitch I fold up into the snow and look back through the swirling cloud as the ghostly figure of a shattered climber materialises at the other end of the rope."

They find a place to pitch tents for the night, and to their horror wake up to find snow falling, blending into the cloud so that nothing has shape or form. Should they give up again, or press on and face the danger of walking over the side of the mountain?

They decide to go ahead, playing a game of blind man's buff as they pick their way along the ridge to the summit slopes, in intense cold and hampered by loose snow.

At 7am that morning they reach the summit. "No fantastic summit views, just photographs of misty backgrounds."

But a triumph all the same. Another example of man's determination to pit himself against Nature.

The expedition was now an unqualified success. They had climbed the two peaks that they had set out to conquer. They had even found a name for Point 20,300: 'Devachen', a word from Buddhist mythology, meaning 'the paradise of boundless light'.

They could sit back well content with themselves and enjoy a brief rest in the magnificent surroundings. But they still had one week's rations left and they all had the spirit of adventure. They had conquered two of the peaks of their

The Mountaineering Challenge

Himalayan Trilogy—so why not use the spare week to try out a new, difficult route up the third?

Papsura, the highest peak in the area, had already been climbed by a previous British expedition but the 1977 team aimed to try a bold, new route.

Barry Needle and Rowland Merriment set off on 31 May to camp at the base of Papsura ready to set out the next morning.

They set off early up steep connecting snowfields to the shoulder. Several hundred feet of difficult climbing followed until they reached a crest of rock at the foot of a high ridge.

The ridge proved tougher than expected.

"The ridge appeared as a steep tower which when climbed only fell back to reveal another tower and then another. The rock was sound granite, warm to the touch with occasional patches of snow, but giving very delicate climbing on short walls and steep slabs, all proving harder than expected."

Despite the problems, they climbed hard for the rest of the day until they reached the area where they had thought they might be able to pitch a tent for the night. It was hopeless—too steep and impractical. So they had no choice but to press on, tired and cold. At that point they came on what they feared most: an impasse. It took them two hours to climb 60 feet, and the route ahead still didn't look any easier. Darkness was falling and still no place even to bivouac, let alone pitch a tent. The climb was proving desperately hard. Finally, in fading light, they saw a suitable ledge beneath a large overhang, and made for it.

From Barry Needle's description, it was hardly an attractive place to pass the night: "The ledge proved to be a level area about three feet wide. Too small for the

The camera captures two expedition members approaching the assault camp, at 18,500 feet, for 'Devachen' (Point 20,300).

tent, but it would have to do. Knocking several pitons into the rock to secure us and our equipment, we pulled on our sleeping bags and sat down on what insulation we could find. I lit the stove, it went out. I tried again; it was too cold and the paraffin wouldn't vap-

orise. . . . After one hour I handed Rowland a cup of melted snow with sugar and milk in it and it went down without comment.

". . . Rowland sat on the ledge in his sleeping bag, his feet in his rucksack, hanging over the edge. I managed to stretch out luxuriously, in the process of which I knocked the bag of milk over the edge into the darkness."

The final ascent the next day was easier than expected, and by 1pm they had conquered the third summit of their Himalayan Trilogy. They decided to try a new route down from the summit. They had only just set off when it started to snow. Soon their visibility was almost nil and their helmets were caked with ice.

In desperately difficult conditions they continued their slow and careful descent. Suddenly a hissing noise reached them. Fresh snow which was still falling heavily was coming down the slope in powder avalanches. There was nothing for it but to dig in their axes and lean away from the avalanche to avoid being swept off the slope and carried down the mountain. More and larger avalanches followed, and it was not until 8pm that they reached the comparative safety of the Papsura glacier and stumbled towards a safe, flat area on which to pitch their tent.

Of the three climbs, Papsura is rated the most difficult according to the official grading system. But none of the peaks was easy, and all presented unknown hazards.

Perhaps some idea of why they do it can be gleaned from Paul Bean's comment after he had climbed Point 20,300. Exhausted, wet and even in pain, he finds his emotions are mixed as he stands at the top.

He says: "Perhaps later I'll be able to remember some of the good times and less of the bad. Photographs are good for doing just that, but no success is worth reliving unless it was achieved with difficulty."

The Mountaineering Challenge
Annapurna Climb

A member of the 1970 Annapurna South Face Expedition, Clough, photographed by colleague Chris Bonington, negotiating the Ice Ridge, at 22,000 feet.

The two men in the sleeping bags stirred. From the holes in the tops of the bags, frost-rimmed heads emerged, moustaches and beards white with snow and ice.

They looked at one another and looked at the sky. The weather had improved but it was far from perfect. From time to time cloud obscured the scene and the neighbouring peaks. Jets of flying snow and ice spurted uncertainly in all directions. And it was cold, very cold.

What lay ahead? As the clouds briefly parted, they could see a snow ridge above them with an ice-field leading up to it. Beyond lay an 800-foot climb to the summit of one of the world's greatest mountains: Annapurna.

They made up their minds to press on. The ice-field was not too difficult, the snow ridge presented no problems, but the climb beyond was quite another matter.

Some of the walls were vertical or even leaning backwards. Each man concentrated on his own climbing, lost in a silent world in which every now and then all sight and sound would be blotted out by a flurry of snow.

The second man was having difficulty. Once, twice, three times his right crampon came off and he had to stop, hanging on to the cliff wall like a demented fly, fixing the errant straps with one free hand, whilst the other hand retained his link with life itself.

Fifty feet from the top there was trouble. The mountain wall appeared to be made up of big flat rocks, but careful scraping revealed that some of them were very insubstantial things of frozen snow which crumbled at the touch and went helter-skeltering down the mountainside towards the base, 26,000 feet below.

There was nothing for it but to examine each 'rock' in the path carefully before making the next move.

This done, no barriers remained, and the two scrambled on to the summit of Annapurna to find some comparatively large, flat spaces running down into the cloud but mercifully sheltered from the wind.

Don Whillans and Dougal Haston had climbed the South Face of Annapurna. It was May 1970.

They still had to get back to their camp below. They used a fixed rope and although Dougal again had trouble with the crampon which had bothered him on the ascent, they made it safely. They switched on their radio link with the Base Camp to hear the expedition leader ask anxiously, "Did you manage to get out today?" "Yes," came the laconic reply, "we just climbed Annapurna."

The Explorers

Thor Heyerdahl's *Ra II*, successor to *Kon-Tiki,* was built in Egypt of papyrus held together with rope. Heyerdahl successfully sailed her from Africa to America to prove that men could have made the journey 2000 years ago.

Kon-Tiki

Did the Incas of South America cross the Pacific Ocean and settle in the South Seas? Thor Heyerdahl, a Norwegian studying primitive peoples, believed that they did, but when he put his theory to other academics and anthropologists, they poured scorn on it.

On the face of it, it did seem unlikely that they could have made such an immense voyage with only the frail craft at their disposal. But there were so many signs which suggested to Heyerdahl that there was a link between the two cultures, that he refused to be put off his theory, even when he couldn't get any support for it.

In the end, he decided that there was only one way to prove it: make the journey himself, using only the sort of boat which the Incas would have had in about 1100 AD; and that meant crossing the Pacific from Peru to the South Sea Islands on a balsa wood raft!

He found five other men who were willing to accompany him, and they set about constructing the raft. This was a task in itself! It was assembled using the original methods and materials which would have been used by the Incas. Nine balsa logs from the Ecuador jungle formed the base. A small cabin was constructed from bamboo canes, a steering oar and a square sail were made, and the raft was complete. Among the essential provisions of food and water was a radio for communication, and a rubber dinghy which later proved essential.

They named their raft *Kon-Tiki* after the sun god of Inca legends, and the legendary ancestor Tiki thought by the Polynesian islanders to have come from the East (one of the many links that Heyerdahl found between the cultures).

They departed from Calloa, Peru, on 28 May 1947. The raft was their home for the next 101 days.

Would it become waterlogged and sink? Could it cope with the high seas and cross currents? These were questions which they anxiously asked themselves as they set off. The raft was soon to prove itself seaworthy after surviving treacherously rough waters.

Food was no problem as the deck was continually festooned with flying fish that had accidentally hit the raft on descent, after leaping from the sea. They were not the only visitors. 'Snake fish' three feet in length and bearing a mouthful of long, sharp teeth were not such desirable company.

They were also wary of octopus as they had been warned that the octopus might surface at night and find their way aboard the raft. So the men always kept a knife close at hand ready to release themselves in the event of waking to find themselves in the tight grip of one of these powerful creatures.

They sighted whales a number of times, and on one occasion several of these huge creatures swam alongside the raft. It would have taken very little effort for a whale to have upturned the entire raft, so it was a very unnerving experience for the crew, but fortunately the whales ignored them. So long as none of the crew interfered with them, they were no danger.

The 'whale shark'—the largest shark known, with an average length of 50 feet—was another unwelcome visitor. They feared it might attack them, and its 15 tons of weight would certainly have wrecked their frail craft.

While some of the crew were bathing in the peaceful waters one day, a number of blue sharks put in

an appearance, and had the crew scrambling for the raft. The sharks made no attempt to attack, but the ferocity with which they mauled scraps thrown into the sea left the expedition members in no doubt of their viciousness.

They didn't make contact with any other vessels during their days at sea. At the halfway stage, 2000 miles away from South America and the same distance from the Polynesian Islands, they had only dolphins for company.

Though parts of the voyage were calm, there were moments when the tempestuous seas and storms threatened to engulf the boat.

But one of their most dangerous moments came when they had sighted land. They were well aware of the obstacle which lay in their way: the waves were hitting against a coral reef which lay below the water and caused huge, rough seas. Waves 25 feet high pounded down, battering the crew. They dared not allow themselves to be swept overboard for fear of the razor sharp corals below. Each man clung for support to part of the raft, choosing the section which he personally felt to be the most secure. Astonishingly, no life was lost. Once the raft had drifted far enough towards land, all six men were able to leave the *Kon-Tiki*—now virtually a wreck, but still afloat—and wade across the remainder of the reef to an uninhabited island.

A few days later they were found by friendly Polynesians from a nearby island, and were able to return to civilisation.

Although some people still doubted Heyerdahl's theory, he had proved beyond doubt that the Incas would have been able to make that incredible voyage.

The Explorers
Amundsen and Scott

In the history of Polar exploration, two names in particular stand out amongst those of many fine and brave people: Norway's Roald Amundsen and Britain's Captain Scott.

Amundsen gained his early experience with other people's expeditions and he was a member of the Belgian Antarctic Expedition of 1897-99, the first to spend a winter south of the Antarctic Circle.

Then he became fired with the idea of being the first to reach the North Pole, but he was forestalled by Dr. Cook and Commander Peary (doubts have since been cast on their claims, but Amundsen did not know that at the time).

He turned his attention to the South Pole and again found that he had a race on his hands. The British, with an expedition led by Captain Scott, were also trying to reach the objective.

Scott was following a route to the polar plateau known as the Beardmore Glacier, which had been discovered by another British explorer, Ernest Shackleton. So Amundsen decided to head south and find his own route over completely uncharted territory.

He could have been unlucky and found some insuperable barrier such as an unbroken mountain range; but in fact he was lucky and found a route across the Axel Heiberg Glacier.

Although he made light of it afterwards, it involved a tremendous feat of climbing. And at the end of it, he was the first man ever to reach the South Pole. The date was 14 December 1911.

Scott and his four companions arrived just a month later, to find that they had been forestalled by Amundsen. To them, it was

Above: Captain Scott (centre) and his crew at the foot of Mount Erebus, in Antarctica, during their ill-fated expedition to the South Pole.

Left: Roald Amundsen pictured during his successful expedition in 1911 to reach the South Pole.

a terrible blow. So much suffering, so much effort, only to be beaten.

Scott wrote in his diary:

"Great God. This is an awful place and terrible enough for us to have laboured to it, without the reward of priority."

Scott's return journey ended in total tragedy. He and his four courageous companions all perished in the icy wastes of the Antarctic.

Exploration— By Hovercraft

The old world and the new meet as a lone African peacefully paddles his canoe in a West African backwater, while a giant hovercraft skims across the vast stretch of main river. The hovercraft was part of an expedition that in 1969 took 65 days to cross 7000 miles of West Africa. On board were scientists, geographers and engineers, whose aim was to increase their own particular fields of knowledge about the region. The hovercraft's unique qualities have enabled previously unexplored areas to be opened up for study.

The Explorers
The Zaire Expedition

The Zaire River, formerly the River Congo, flows through its vast basin, through swamp and dense jungle, down cataract and rapid, and until recently it had remained largely unexplored, never having been navigated from its source to the sea.

One of the most daring explorations of the river had been by Henry Morton Stanley in 1874. He set off with 350 native bearers, only 115 of whom survived the journey. He began his exploration 600 miles below the source of the river and completed the remaining 2118 miles in 11 months. He was attacked, ambushed and had to fight disease as well as the unfriendly people around, so it was regarded as a triumph for him that he survived at all.

In 1974, just one hundred years later, a team set off not only to

explore the river, but to make scientific surveys along its full length, one of the most important being a study of River Blindness—a tropical eye disease.

They had the benefits of modern equipment and technology, but it was still a daring undertaking.

Specially adapted inflatable boats and water-jet craft were used to navigate the river, and were found to be ideal for the cataracts and rapids. Since there are 32 individual cataracts between Kinshasa and Matadi, it was necessary to be equipped to face them!

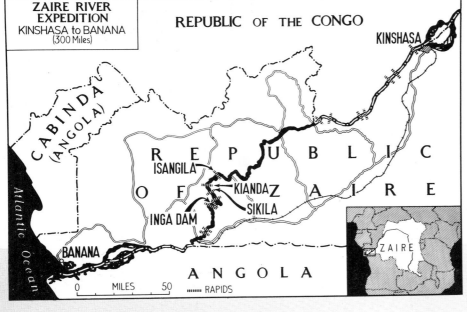

ZAIRE RIVER EXPEDITION
KINSHASA to BANANA
(300 Miles)

REPUBLIC OF THE CONGO

KINSHASA

CABINDA (ANGOLA)

Atlantic Ocean

R E P U B L I C   O F   Z A I R E

ISANGILA
KIANDAZ
SIKILA
INGA DAM

BANANA

ANGOLA

0   MILES   50   RAPIDS

ZAIRE

Above: All the occupants were thrown from this craft at one time or another as they negotiated 15 miles of rough water, between Kolwezi and the infamous Red Gorge. The stretch of water included a series of perilous African rapids. This was only the third time that anyone had attempted this stretch of the river. The 1974 expedition was carried out to commemorate Stanley's exploration of the river 100 years previously.

Right: Members of the expedition hurtle down a treacherous mile-long stretch of rapids near Kolwezi. Holes were torn in four boats as they negotiated this stretch. Buffeted by strong currents, the boats were thrown on to submerged rocks. Further down the river *La Vision*, one of the craft, careered over another submerged boulder and pitched into a 14-foot hole in the river at Bamanga. Four of the boats were sucked into the swirling pit, and then catapulted like shuttlecocks into a calm stretch of the river.

The Explorers
Secrets of the Welsh Caves

When Eileen Davies, a domestic science teacher, started out to wriggle her way through a passage that was at times no more than a foot high, nobody knew what she would find at the end of it—or, indeed, whether it would end in an impassable barrier.

But Eileen was determined to find out, for she was a member of the South Wales Caving Club, and they were exploring a previously unexplored section at the back of the Black Caves.

The passage that she was working her way through was known as Endless Crawl; many potholers had tried to explore it before her but had turned back, losing heart and nerve in the rib-crushing confines of the Crawl.

So you want to start caving? (or potholing as it is more usually known in the north of England). Then join one of the caving clubs which operate under the auspices of the National Caving Association, and learn the techniques of good, safe caving from the start. You will need a helmet, a lamp, boots, and old, warm clothes. Clubs will supply ladders, ropes and other equipment. The main caving areas in England are the Yorkshire Dales, the Derbyshire Peak District, South Wales and the Mendip Hills in Somerset.

Above: Progress when potholing is often difficult. Here an enthusiast negotiates a streamway in the Bakerloo Straight, which is too narrow for a boat.

Right: Half a mile beyond Flabbergasm Chasm the party found this roaring cascade, 100 feet high, overhanging the entrance to Hanger Passage, and with another waterfall 60 feet above it.

Far left: Potholing demands many skills and a great deal of courage and resolution. Here in Go Slow Passage one of the potholers shows that one also needs to be something of a mountaineer!

Left: Eileen Davies wriggles out of the end of the Endless Crawl—the first person to brave the 350-foot narrow, black passage, often only 12 inches high.

Eileen didn't lose heart or nerve, and because of her courage it is now known that the tunnel is 350 feet long, and opens out into a breathtakingly beautiful scene.

Blood-red stalagmites several feet high dot the floors of caves, and ten-foot straws (pencil-thin stalactites) hang from the roof. Further on there is a crystal pool fringed with flower-like calcite formations, a canal of dark green water, mysterious and deep, and a 100-foot waterfall which cascades down the rock.

In places, the roof rises like a Norman arch to a height of 50 feet. So excited were the team by their discoveries that they named one chasm Flabbergasm Chasm, a name which perfectly expresses the excitement and wonder of that first discovery.

Once Eileen Davies had braved the unknown, dark and narrow tunnel, and had found the way through, others followed. But it takes a special kind of courage to be the first.

Wings

1910: Claude Graham-White and a lady passenger flying in a Henri Farman biplane.

Charles Lindbergh

One of the most famous pioneers of early flying was Charles Lindbergh, an American who was the first to fly single-handed across the Atlantic.

Later he became world famous as the man whose son was the tragic victim of a brutal kidnapping case.

Charles Lindbergh was a schoolboy during the First World War, and became interested in flying through reading an Edgar Wallace serial about a wartime fighter pilot.

Once he had learned to fly, he earned his living performing aerial stunts in a battered old wartime plane. When the Government became aware of the commercial possibilities of the aeroplane, Lindbergh became one of the first airmail flyers. While he was working as an airmail pilot, a prize was put up for the first pilot to fly non-stop from New York to London, and Lindbergh determined to have a

Louis Bleriot, the French airman, pictured the day after his historic flight across the Channel from Dover to Calais on 25 July 1909, the first time the Channel had been crossed by air.

Huge crowds surged around the *Spirit of St. Louis* when it arrived in Brussels after Lindbergh had flown it across the Atlantic from New York to Paris, in the first ever solo transatlantic flight.

go. In a single-engined monoplane, *The Spirit of St. Louis,* without radio or parachute, he took off from New York shortly after dawn on the morning of 20 May 1927. Thirty-three and a half hours later he landed in Paris. He was 25 years old, and a hero.

Wings
Famous Test Pilots

Neville Duke

Neville Duke

Like many test pilots, Neville Duke began his flying career with the RAF during the war. He had wanted to be an airman from the day that he had his first five-shilling ride at an air circus which visited his home in Kent.

On joining the RAF in 1940 he was posted to Biggin Hill and by 1941 was piloting Spitfires. Then he was posted to North Africa and later was given command of a squadron during the Italian campaign. When he returned to England in 1944 he was the holder of the D.S.O., D.F.C. and two bars, having shot down 28 enemy aircraft. He had made 486 sorties and flown 712 hours on operational flights—and he was still only 22 years old.

He took the test pilots' course and, on leaving the RAF in 1948, joined Hawker Aircraft, becoming chief test pilot in 1951.

He is most associated with the Hawker Hunter, in which he established a new world record in 1953 with speeds of 741 miles an hour on two runs.

He had a lucky escape in 1955 when he had engine failure over Littlehampton. Knowing that he could not reach his base at Tangmere he decided to try and land on Thorney Island. The plane kept bouncing, so he decided to pull the undercarriage up and land that way. The plane careered along the runway on her belly, hurtled through a hedge, over a ditch, and smashed into the sea wall. Duke broke his back and was off flying for four months. But it didn't put him off for good. He was back at work again as soon as he was fit.

Tom Brooke-Smith

Unlike the other test pilots, Tom Brooke-Smith learned to fly before the war, at Brooklands. He spent the war as a test pilot and in 1948 was appointed Chief Test Pilot to Shorts. He was responsible for the early work on the Short SC1 vertical take-off aircraft. The SC1 was a new concept in flying and introduced new horrors for the test pilot. Unlike an autogyro, it relied on the thrust of the jet engines to lift it from the ground; and the pilot knew that if the engines failed he would come down like a stone. The transition from vertical to horizontal flight required great skill, knowledge and calmness from the pilot.

Peter Twiss

Peter Twiss, test pilot for Fairey Aviation, served in the Fleet Air Arm during the war, and had a distinguished war record.

His moment of greatest triumph with Fairey's came in 1956 when he set up the World Absolute Speed Record of 1,132 mph. This beat the previous record by the fantastic margin of 310 mph!

At that time, he had flown 140 different types of plane, and had piloted more high-performance aircraft than any other Englishman.

In recent years he has been a prominent powerboat racer.

Peter Twiss

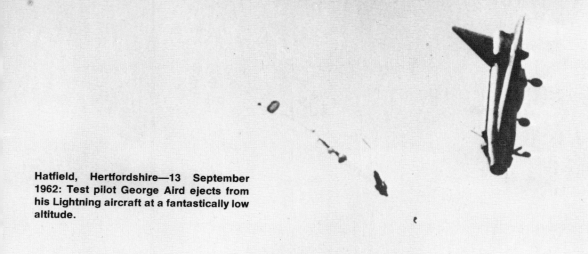

Hatfield, Hertfordshire—13 September 1962: Test pilot George Aird ejects from his Lightning aircraft at a fantastically low altitude.

Wings

Roland 'Bee' Beamont

Roland 'Bee' Beamont

Roland 'Bee' Beamont learned to fly when he entered the RAF in 1938. As a Hurricane fighter pilot in France and in the Battle of Britain he shot down five enemy aircraft. Later he flew Typhoons and Tempests, and by the end of the war had flown 630 operational hours on 441 combat flights. He was credited with eight enemy aircraft shot down, four probably destroyed, five damaged, thirty-two flying bombs destroyed and a minesweeper and thirty-five trains damaged.

As a civilian test pilot he was on the maiden flights of four outstanding British aircraft: the Canberra, Britain's first jet bomber; the P.1, Britain's first supersonic aircraft; the Lightning, Britain's first supersonic fighter; and the TSR 2, an advanced tactical strike and reconnaissance aircraft.

He was the first British pilot to exceed Mach 1 in a British aircraft in level flight; made the first flight by a British aircraft at Mach 2; and set three Atlantic records in the Canberra. His achievements won him considerable recognition, including many trophies, and the C.B.E., D.S.O. and Bar, D.F.C. and Bar, and U.S.D.F.C.

Brian Trubshaw

Brian Trubshaw is a name associated by most people with Concorde, the Anglo-French supersonic airliner.

Trubshaw served with the RAF from 1942 to 1950, then joined Vickers Armstrong as experimental test pilot.

He became Chief Test Pilot in 1960.

Before the Concorde project began, Trubshaw had been responsible for the development of several successful airliners—the VC10, Super VC10 and three versions of the BAC 1-11.

He was closely connected with Concorde from its inception in 1965 and took it up for its first flight in 1969.

The most famous woman flyer of post-war years is solo pilot Sheila Scott, who, following the tradition of the early fliers such as Amy Johnson and Jean Batten, has set many single-engine records.

In 1966 she set a new round-the-world air speed record for women. Flying a Piper Comanche, she took 33 days for her epic flight and averaged 36 miles an hour, including ground stops. Left: Sheila Scott stepping from the cockpit on arrival at London Airport after her record-breaking flight.

Death of a Test Pilot

Saturday, 6 September 1952, was a grey overcast day, but the weather did not deter 120,000 spectators determined to see the Farnborough Air Show.

The big attraction was a flight by the experimental De Havilland 110 in which John Derry, the first Briton to break the sound barrier four years earlier, was to break the sound barrier yet again, with observer Tony Richards.

The aircraft was of twin-boom design, fifty-three feet long and powered by two Rolls-Royce Avon jet engines, each of them capable of more than three tons of thrust.

On that eventful Saturday, Derry and Richards boarded their plane, made all the usual checks and took off from Hatfield for the short flight to Farnborough.

Excitement among the vast crowd was intense as the public address system announced that the DH110 was approaching at 40,000 feet and would soon begin the dive which would take it through the sound barrier.

Miles above the airfield, Derry pushed the stick forward with throttles wide open and the plane went into its high-speed dive. Seconds later came the double clap of thunder which indicated that the plane had broken the sound barrier.

Derry levelled out and began a high-speed low-level pass in front of the crowd, turned, and passed behind the control tower and approached the airfield again.

Then came disaster. The plane disintegrated in mid-air. Then came even worse horror.

The engines, torn adrift from the body of the aircraft but still impelled by their own tremendous power, hurtled towards the crowd. One, thankfully, did nothing worse than smash through the roof of a hangar. The other hit the ground and scythed through the thick mass of people on Observation Hill. It wreaked death and destruction all along its path, exploding like a bomb. Into the carnage smashed the front of the plane with Derry and Richards still strapped in, although killed the instant the plane disintegrated.

There was an awful silence. Then the screams and shouts and sirens began.

Twenty-nine spectators were killed and sixty injured on that dreadful day.

The aircraft that Derry and Richards were flying was to become the famous Sea Vixen fighter in service aboard the Fleet Air Arm's carriers.

Wings
Concorde: A New Era

When Concorde flew on its first test flight, there was 12 tons of special instrumentation aboard to check every detail of the aircraft's performance.

This gives some idea of the enormous developments that there have been in the aircraft industry since the first tiny planes took off from small fields less than a century ago.

The pioneers of flight were brave men who risked their lives to further mankind's knowledge of flying. But there is just as much

Brian Trubshaw (left) and John Cochrane pictured at the controls of Concorde.

danger for the modern test pilot. Our knowledge of the technological problems has advanced each year, but in some ways this only increases the danger for the test pilot.

In developing Concorde, the designers and engineers were working on the frontiers of technical knowledge. It took more than a decade of research and 5000 hours of flight development before the first prototype, the 01, was ready for its first test flight. During the test flights, the aircraft is pushed way beyond the limitations of normal flight requirements, in order to find any snags which might occur under abnormal operating conditions, and this, too, increases the element of danger.

Fortunately for test pilot André Turcat Concorde handled well on its first test in March 1969, and after the first supersonic tests the following October, all the pilots who had flown Concorde reported that the plane was easy to handle and presented no major problems.

This was a great relief to the designers, who had had many anxious moments during the period of research and development.

Concorde was a joint project by Britain and France. For some years, Britain had been considering the possibility of developing a supersonic airliner. There were already many military planes capable of supersonic flight, but they usually stayed supersonic for only relatively short periods. The problems of designing a passenger craft which would cruise at speeds greater than sound were enormous.

It was decided that Britain could not develop such a plane alone, and approaches were made to other countries. France had been thinking along similar lines, and so the liaison between two great companies—British Aircraft Corporation (BAC) in England and Aérospatiale in France—was begun.

Many major decisions had to be made in the early stages. Should the aircraft be swing-wing like the military planes or fixed-wing like other airliners? What material should be used for the main structure?

The final choice, made only after exhaustive studies, was for a slender delta shape wing, and for an aluminium alloy for the basic structural material. This, too, was only chosen after long and careful tests of all the available materials.

One of the first things people notice about Concorde is its drooping nose, and this, too, was decided on after design studies of various configurations to give the pilots maximum visibility while maintaining a streamlined surface in flight. The 'droop snoot', as it has been called, offers the best of all worlds. With the nose down the pilot and co-pilot have better visibility for take-off and landing than is offered by most modern jet airliners, but after take-off the nose is lifted so that it is nearly in line with the body, and it goes still higher to present a completely streamlined surface when the plane is travelling at supersonic speeds.

Among the many problems faced by Concorde's designers, which had not been met by other aircraft designers, was that of temperature. Their plane would have to cope with temperatures which would vary from minus 45°C when flying at subsonic speeds in the icy upper atmosphere, to 150°C plus in supersonic flight.

Concorde is designed to cruise at Mach 2 (1350 mph), which means that it can make the trip from Paris to Washington in three and a half hours. This is highly significant to businessmen who cross the Atlantic regularly, since a saving in time is a saving in money to them. And the short flight time saves them from the problems of jet lag.

It cost a lot of money to develop Concorde—about £1000 million. This was because the designers were trying to do something which had not been done before and for which there were no precedents in design or marketing.

Their solutions to the problems have been widely acclaimed as brilliant even by people who are opposed to supersonic airliners. In producing Concorde they have ushered in a new era in air travel, and one whose significance will be felt for decades to come.

Wheels

The First Racers

Motor racing and danger go together. Too many young men have died on the track for anyone to be in doubt about the dangers of this exciting sport. Yet there are always more drivers ready to take the place of those who are killed, risking their necks for the challenge of proving their skill against other drivers.

In the early days of motor racing, many of these young men were rich, and raced for amusement. Speeds were nothing like the speeds of modern racing, but it was still a dangerous sport.

The motoring world has never stopped arguing about the world's first race. Some say that it was won by the Comte de Dion in 1894 and others by Levassor in 1895.

What is certain is that in December 1893 the French newspaper *Le Petit Journal* announced a competition over a route from Paris to Rouen, a distance of 78.5 miles. But there were frequent halts for the drivers to take refreshment and for the cars to be shown to the public, so many historians claim that it was a rally, not a race.

The first car to reach Rouen was a De Dion steam-drag, driven by the Comte de Dion at an average of 11.6 mph. But because he had a mechanic to deal with the steam boiler, he was disqualified.

The following year an undisputed race was held from Paris to Bordeaux and back again, a distance of 732 miles.

Twenty cars started, thirteen petrol-driven, six steam and one electric. Nine finished, eight of them petrol-driven and the other steam-driven. First home was Emile Levassor, at an average speed of 15 mph, but, like the Comte de Dion, he was disqualified on a technicality.

Next to stage a competition were the Americans in 1895. Britain did not enter the motor racing scene until much later because of the restrictions placed by the Government on the use of cars on the highway. Even when S. F. Edge won the international Gordon Bennett race in 1902, giving Britain the right to stage the race in 1903, the Government refused to relent and the race was staged in Southern Ireland.

Not until 1907 did motor racing come into its own in Great Britain, when the famous Brooklands track was opened at Weybridge in Surrey.

Wheels

The Early Days

The Second World War provided something of a watershed for motor racing. Before 1939 the drivers were often rich amateurs who raced for the sheer thrill of it. After 1945 came a more dedicated, professional breed of racer.

There was a big change for Britain too, since British manufacturers now produced cars to match the world's best—Cooper, Vanwall, BRM, Lotus, Brabham, McLaren, Tyrrell and many more.

With the new cars came many new, eager British and Commonwealth drivers. Men such as Mike Hawthorn, Peter Collins, Graham Hill, John Surtees, Stirling Moss, Jim Clark, Jackie Stewart, Denny Hulme, Bruce McLaren, Innes Ireland and, latterly, James Hunt.

But it is arguable that the greatest racing driver of all time was an Argentinian, Juan Manuel Fangio. Although he did not make his European debut until he was 38, Fangio notched up ten wins in 1950, four more in 1951, two in 1952, three in 1953, six the following year, seven in 1955, six in 1956, ten again in 1957 and one (back home in Buenos Aires) in 1958, after which he retired from racing, prosperous and respected.

It was in the 1960s that Britain's racing drivers really came to the fore. Men like Hawthorn, Hill, Surtees, Clark, Stewart and Hunt have all been World Champion, yet the man many think was the best British driver ever—Stirling Moss—never won that honour. He broke into racing just after the war when the Italians, Germans and French still ruled the roost. He didn't get a real opportunity until 1955 when he drove as No. 2 to Fangio in the Mercedes team and won the British Grand Prix. The same year, he won the Mille Miglia, the Targa Florio and Tourist Trophy, a hat-trick of

Wheels

Above: Frank Newton (in car) and S. F. Edge photographed at Brooklands in the early days of racing.

Left: John Cobb's Napier-Railton at speed on the banking at Brooklands. Cobb later turned to water speed records, and was tragically killed on Loch Ness in 1952 during one such attempt.

Right: Jack Brabham seconds before he retired from the 1961 Monaco Grand Prix.

the world's oldest races.

After this, the British cars came along and he drove to victory in Vanwall, Lotus and Cooper cars, but always the world title eluded him. Once (in Mike Hawthorn's championship year) he lost by only one point.

Moss retired in 1962 after a bad crash at Goodwood.

Jim Clark, a dark, quiet Scottish farmer, became world champion in 1963 with a record seven Grand Prix victories, one more than the previous best by Fangio and Ascari. He was champion again in 1965 with six wins. In 1968 he created another record by notching up his 25th major Grand Prix victory when he won the South African Grand Prix, but he was killed shortly afterwards in a minor race in Germany.

A contrast to Jim Clark was the extrovert personality of Graham Hill. He was already 28 years old when he began racing in 1957. He won the title with BRM in 1962, was runner-up in 1963, 1964 and

1965, then rejoined Lotus to take the title again. Hill retired from motor racing, only to be killed in a flying accident while piloting a light plane in bad weather.

The Commonwealth produced its own crop of brilliant drivers, amongst them Jack Brabham, Denny Hulme and Bruce McLaren.

Now a new generation of drivers contest the Grands Prix. The names of the drivers may be different, but the name of the game is still the same: WINNING.

Superstitions

The photographer had a deadline to meet, but racing driver 'Red' Campbell hesitated. One of the strongest superstitions of the racing track is that it is unlucky to be photographed just before a race begins.

Finally, he gave in. "OK," he said, "take your picture."

Sixty seconds later he had driven his last race as he piled up in a holocaust of molten metal.

Another superstition is that it is unlucky to have a woman or child in the car, and the other drivers shook their heads in disbelief when they saw 38-year-old Australian Bill Sleman jogging his daughter up and down on his lap in the cockpit of his car. A few minutes later, he rounded a bend at 70 miles an hour, mounted the bank, turned over and rolled back into the road. The crash had killed him outright.

'Doc' Mackenzie was something of a character, easily distinguishable on the race track because of his dark, luxuriant beard. He always declared that he would shave it off when he won the big 500 race at Indianapolis, and not a day before. So everyone was surprised when he turned up one

day smooth-chinned and minus his characteristic beard. "Just got married," he mumbled. "Wife didn't like the beard."

Friends feared that he was tempting Providence, and sure enough he crashed and was killed in the first race of the day.

There are many other superstitions surrounding the racing driver. Many drivers have their own 'lucky charm', and, of course, the most universal of these is the medallion of St. Christopher.

In a sport as dangerous as motor racing, it is hardly surprising that they try to bring themselves just that extra bit of luck.

Wheels

Motor Racing Today

'Motor Racing Is Dangerous'. That chilly reminder is printed on every motor racing admission ticket sold in the British Isles.

No one knows the risks and dangers more than Niki Lauda, the 1977 World Champion. The Austrian driver was badly burned when his scarlet Ferrari crashed during the 1976 German Grand Prix at the Nurburgring circuit. His condition was critical for several days, flames from blazing fuel having attacked his face and seared his lungs. Lauda recovered but the horrifying accident did not seem to deter him. Within six weeks he had returned to the wheel of his Ferrari; one year later he had clinched the World Championship for the second time.

Lauda had demonstrated one of the most important qualities of a racing driver—determination to win. His mother and father had tried to persuade him to give up any ideas of becoming a racing driver, but Niki was determined. He borrowed money from a bank and took up motor racing seriously. Eventually he was invited to join the Ferrari Grand Prix team with whom he won many Grands Prix plus the World Championship in 1975 and 1977.

The Formula One World Championship is the pinnacle of motor racing. The battle is fought over as many as 17 different circuits scattered throughout the world. Tracks range from fast man-made circuits in South Africa and Austria to tight, brutal street circuits in California and Monaco.

Formula One teams design and construct their own cars. Travel and manufacturing costs are high and teams work with cigarette manufacturers, petrol and oil companies, banks and other commercial concerns who sponsor the teams in return for advertising space on the cars.

As much as 40 gallons of petrol are required for a car to run the non-stop 200-mile Grand Prix. As a result, the driver sits in a reclined position at the front of the car with the fuel tanks located behind him as well as on either side of the cockpit.

Fire is one of the biggest hazards in motor racing and the fuel is carried in tanks that are constructed of foam and rubber in an effort to prevent spillage in an accident.

Drivers dress in flame-proof underwear, overalls, socks and gloves. A flame-proof balaclava face-mask is worn under a full-face crash helmet. In addition, an air line is attached to the helmet to provide the driver with oxygen in the event of fire. With the aid of such useful equipment, a driver can survive in a fire for about one minute without suffering major burns.

Grand Prix cars are capable of speeds of over 175 mph thanks to their powerful engines and smooth shape. The force of air passing over the body and large rear wing keeps the machine firmly on the track. The engine is mounted at the rear and power is transmitted through the fat rear tyres.

Racing tyres are constructed without treads for the dry condi-

tions. The smooth rubber surface heats up and becomes sticky, thus giving the car grip. But smooth tyres are useless in wet conditions. Tyres with treads or 'grooves' (similar to those found on a family saloon car) are essential for a wet track.

Driving at speed under various weather conditions requires skill, and drivers learn the art of motor racing in the junior classes or 'formulae'. Britain's James Hunt is a fine example of a driver who has progressed from racing a Mini to driving a Formula One car. James won the World Championship in 1976 after a thrilling battle to the very last race with Niki Lauda. Hunt drives for the Marlboro-McLaren team and he is considered to be one of the fastest drivers in Grand Prix racing.

One of his toughest opponents is the American, Mario Andretti, who races with the John Player-sponsored Lotus team. Andretti was born in Italy but his family moved to North America where Mario competed in many different classes of racing before turning to Grand Prix racing.

The Lotus Grand Prix team is one of the most experienced in motor racing. During the past fifteen years, Lotus have won the Drivers' World Championship five times and their experience is surpassed only by that of Ferrari.

The famous Italian team have been racing since 1948 and they are the only team to manufacture their own engines. Other Formula One teams rely generally on the Ford Grand Prix engine.

Grand Prix teams have a tough schedule to maintain. Two days of practice precede every grand Prix. Drivers circulate on the track in an effort to set the fastest lap and earn 'pole position' at the front of the starting grid. Competition is unbelievably tough with drivers setting times that are fractions of a second apart.

Between races, the cars are returned to England where most teams are based. Modifications are made to the cars in the search for that vital extra fraction of speed.

Speed is the essence of motor racing and with speed comes danger. The art of motor racing is to drive as quickly as possible without making a mistake that could lead to a nasty accident. Drivers are aware of the dangers in the same way as mountaineers and parachutists are familiar with the hazards of their sport. It is part of the attraction.

A driver gets an enormous satisfaction from winning a Grand Prix. It is almost a case of cheating death. Occasionally, accidents are caused by factors that are out of a driver's control. A tyre may puncture, a sudden downpour can cause havoc and occasionally there is a freak set of circumstances that can take a driver's life.

During the 1977 South African Grand Prix, Welsh driver Tom Pryce crested a brow at over 160 mph to find a marshal running across the track with a fire extinguisher to aid another driver whose car had caught fire. Pryce hit the marshal and received a fatal blow on the head from the fire extinguisher. It was a tragic and unnecessary accident that reminded everyone that motor racing is dangerous.

A pile-up at the Thruxton circuit in 1975.

Wheels

Grand Prix

The Grand Prix of 1968, held on the German Nurburgring circuit, was run in unbelievably bad conditions. Fog was the worst hazard on the first day of practice, but the next day rain proved a bigger menace and one practice session had to be cancelled because the track was too wet and dangerous.

Sunday, the day of the race, was even worse. The fog was still there and the rain was coming down in torrents. The organisers decided upon a special practice session but not many cars turned out for it, and rumour was rife that the race would be called off.

One driver who did turn up for the practice was Jackie Stewart, a Scotsman driving a French car entered by an Englishman. He found that his Matra-Ford was in good shape.

As the time of the race approached there was no sign of a break in the conditions. Water dripped everywhere and the grey, clammy fog blanketed everything so competitors could barely see from one side of the track to the other.

For those who could see through

Above: Jody Scheckter in action during the 1975 German Grand Prix. Born in South Africa, he has not yet won a world championship, although his list of successes is impressive. In 1977 Scheckter notched up first place in three Grand Prix—in Canada, Argentina and Monaco, and took a second in South Africa.

Left: Jackie Stewart brilliantly took the Formula I World Championship three times—in 1969, 1971 and 1973—before retiring at the end of the '73 season.

Right: Ace British racing driver James Hunt careers along on two wheels in his Marlboro-McLaren, after a dramatic five-car pile-up on the first bend of the first lap of the 1976 British Grand Prix at Brands Hatch. The race was stopped for an hour to clear the track, and stewards ruled that drivers who had not completed the first lap—including Hunt—would not be eligible to continue. Hunt did continue, however, and was later ruled to be eligible. Three rival teams then claimed that he should have been disqualified for his part in the crash, but after three hours of deliberation, stewards declared him to be the controversial winner of the race.

the fog, it was a spectacular start with spray flying from the rear wheels as Graham Hill shot to the front, closely followed by Chris Amon of New Zealand and Jackie Stewart. Lashed by the spray from the rear wheels of the cars in front, visibility was almost nil for Stewart, but he pressed hard and succeeded in passing Amon. Then he chased Hill until he had gained the lead. Deep rivers of water ran across the track and it required the greatest concentration to prevent the car aquaplaning.

By the end of the first lap Stewart was eight seconds clear of the field and he increased this to 46 seconds by the end of the third. He continued steadily increasing his lead, circulating like clockwork, so that when the chequered flag fell at the end of fourteen laps Stewart had scored what many described as the greatest classic victory of all time. His winning speed was 86.86 mph (139.8 kph).

Afterwards he said that he nearly did not compete in the race because of an arm injury.

"If the race had been dry I am sure I would not have competed," he said. "In a Formula One car you 'take off' a minimum of 15 times each lap and the strain on your arms and shoulders is considerable due to the extremely high speeds. In the rain this only happens two or three times a lap. My arm did, however, still cause me inconvenience as it was encased in a plaster cast, which made gear-changing and steering awkward."

Has there ever been another man who has won a major Grand Prix with one arm in a plaster cast, and described it as 'an inconvenience'?

The High and the Mighty

Above: 1974: This driver, it seemed, just couldn't stop himself and his Ford from jumping for joy, for plastered all over the car are the names of the fifteen international and national championships this particular model had won during the previous year!

Below: Drag racing is another branch of sport on wheels, and one which has an enthusiastic following. Here you see Clive Skilton's world record-breaking dragster *Revolution 3* off to a scorching start. He covered the 500-metre course in 8.6 seconds.

Wheels
The Story of Speedway

Danger, thrills, spills, speed and colour. These are the ingredients which make up speedway. There is dirt and dust, grease and sweat too, for this is the era of the machine and speedway is a machine-made sport, tailored to a specification of roaring engines and mechanically-minded combatants.

Four riders straddle their machines down there in the pits. Slowly they are wheeled on to the track and up to the starting gate. The dare-devil riders crouch over the handlebars, the starting tapes fly up and the four machines race madly for the first bend, cinders flying in a spume of whirling dust.

Yes, speedway has come a long way since the day in 1923 when the sport was born.

John S. Hoskins was the first man to think of setting machine against machine in a motorcycle race. He announced to the inhabitants of West Maitland in the Hunter River Valley in Australia that he would stage an open motorcycle race meeting, with a first prize of ten pounds. There were forty entrants. Every heat was a handicap and every heat included eight riders. There was no safety-

Above: The art of speedway is the art of broadsiding. The rider in front demonstrates the modern 'foot forward' style. Left: Barry Thomas leads one of the heats for the 1975 *Daily Mirror* open individual speedway event from Ray Wilson (left) and Barry Briggs.

fence and Johnny Hoskins made up the rules as he went along.

Later on, of course, the sport was improved. Safety fences were introduced, the rules formalised. Other tracks soon opened all over Australia, and then, in 1928, the sport came to England for the first time. It had taken over a year to

Two competitors in the 1965 Scramble of the Year at Brands Hatch, Kent, race around the track caked from head to toe in wet mud. And they weren't the only ones. Torrential rain turned the track into a complete quagmire, and *all* the competitors became so mud-spattered that spectators couldn't guess who was who, or even who was winning! But the show must go on, and the enthusiastic and good-tempered scramblers raced on through the sea of mud—for a top prize of £15!

A motorcycle meeting at Crystal Palace on Easter Monday 1969 saw Rose Arnold from Birmingham hurtling around the track in a motorcycle side-car, driven by Norman Hanks. It seems that Rose is not the only woman 'chairing', as it is called; a growing number of enterprising women are taking up the sport.

get permission for the meeting to be held because of the tight restrictions laid down by the Auto Cycle Union, but finally, on 19 February 1928, the dream became a reality.

The organisers expected about 3000 spectators. Thirty thousand arrived. So densely packed was the crowd that the riders raced along narrow lanes between the spectators. The organisers learned their lesson, and the whole track was re-designed before the next meeting, which was held at Easter and attended by 17,000 people.

Other areas soon opened their own tracks and within a few months there were fifty speedway tracks and hundreds of riders competing on them.

The sport was still called 'dirt track' and still bore a strong resemblance to a one-ring circus. Then somebody had the idea of introducing team racing, and that was the beginning of speedway as it is today. The year was 1929, and with the formation of the first Leagues, the sport began to settle down on organised lines.

Teams consisted of four riders and each match comprised six heats. Competitors carried a number on the front of their machines.

Further streamlining came in 1931 when freelances were banned and attempts were made to balance the strength of the teams by pooling the riders and allocating them to different clubs.

Further improvements followed. Clutches were fitted to the bikes and standing starts introduced. Starting gates were installed to prevent disturbances caused by riders jumping the gun. Then the old stripped bikes gave way to two-cylinder models, and these in turn were made obsolete when the modern single-cylinder machine was invented.

Speedway continued to flourish until the outbreak of the Second World War. It came back with a bang after the war when crowds of 80,000 were commonplace, had a prolonged slump, and then revived again.

Today it is Britain's second biggest spectator sport, and a major sport in many other countries including Sweden, Norway, Denmark, Russia, East Germany, Poland, Australia and the United States.

Speedway has never lacked courageous young riders, and those of today are just as daring as the riders of earlier times, risking their lives for the thrill and challenge of speedway.

Wheels

Superstars

Barry Sheene, M.B.E., is the Cockney whizz kid of the Grand Prix motorcycle racing scene. Born in London in 1950, he acquired his passion for motorbikes from his father, Frank 'Franco' Sheene, a maintenance man at the Royal College of Surgeons' Hospital in Holborn, who spent all his spare time preparing motorcycles for the track and attending (with Barry) race meetings in England and Europe.

School was a disaster. Barry left with no qualifications of any sort. He took jobs as a warehouseman, messenger boy (on a motorcycle!) and car cleaner.

His first chance to ride was in the 1968 season at Brands Hatch, where he finished third on a Bultaco in one of his races! The next year, his first full season on the track, he took the lightweight road racing scene by storm, and at 19 years of age finished runner-up in the British 125cc Road Racing Championship. The following season he turned to Suzuki machines and proved unbeatable in the 125cc capacity class, winning the British 125cc Road Racing Championship and taking third place in the 250cc

championship. In the 1971 season he was second in the World Championship; in 1973 he won the European F750 Championship and became 'King of Brands Hatch', 'British Superbike Champion' and was voted 'Man of the Year' by British racing fans.

But his meteoric rise to fame was almost shattered in 1975 when Sheene was severely injured in a dreadful accident, sustained at 180 mph, at Daytona Speedway, Florida, in the opening meeting of the season. Yet only six weeks later he was racing again!—proof of his remarkable courage and love of his sport—and that season he won the Dutch TT and the Swedish Grand Prix.

There was only one title he now wished to gain—World 500cc Road Racing Champion, and this he achieved in 1976 on the RG500 Suzuki, winning every Grand Prix he entered, apart from the Belgian, where he finished second!

In 1977 he took the World Championship again and was awarded the M.B.E.—an honour worthy of one of the greatest road racers of the decade.

2 March 1978: Britain's 18-year-old answer to Evel Knievel, Eddie Kidd, made a daring 145-foot motorcycle leap over a railway ravine, and faced a disastrous 80-foot drop if he failed. The spectacular stunt at Doulting, Somerset, was part of the filming of *Hanover Street,* a new film about the London blitz, in which Eddie stood in for actor Harrison Ford, who was escaping from pursuing Nazis. Strapped to Eddie's back was a dummy representing a pillion passenger, also fleeing. Eddie landed without a crash helmet at 85 mph, and had to fling his 370cc machine on its side to stop. Apart from a cut hand, he was unhurt. He said: "I should have been happier wearing a crash helmet, but I felt reasonably confident wearing my seven lucky charms. I feel I can tackle anything now."

Wheels

There was a moment of triumph for Evel Knievel at Wembley in May 1975, when before a hushed holiday crowd of more than 60,000 people, he jumped over 13 single-decker London buses on his gleaming 750cc Harley Davidson motorcycle.

But, as the series of pictures shows, the attempt ended in disaster, as he crashed on landing on the ramp at 90 mph, to end up pinned beneath the motorbike.

He always has a private ambulance at hand when performing stunts, and on this occasion, it was needed to take him to the London Hospital for immediate treatment to a fractured hand and damaged spine.

24 February 1978: Hurtling through a ring of raging flame is all part of a day's work for the men of the Royal Artillery Motor-cycle Display team. And all part of a day's work, too, for 63-year-old photographer, Freddie Reed. Freddie joined team leader Sergeant Derek Shipley as pillion passenger, and did the stunt twice, hanging on with one hand so that he could keep his camera hand free. The burning, petrol-soaked straw was already falling in their path as Derek's 350cc motorcycle thundered through the tunnel of fire. How did Freddie feel about it? "I like to try something different," he said. "And it's all fun. Derek's confidence in handling his machine on the icy surface was remarkable. All I had to do was hang on to his shirt."

Land and Water

The Campbells

The thrill of going faster than anybody else has attracted many men. But few families have been as closely associated with speed as the Campbells. Starting with Malcolm Campbell in 1924, taken up by his son Donald in 1948, father and son were to make many successful attempts on both land and water speed records, and to dominate the speed scene.

Malcolm Campbell carved out a highly successful business career first, and became a wealthy insurance broker and company director before starting to indulge his passion for speed. When he did start to race, he began with motorbikes, winning his first gold medal in 1906 for the London to Land's End trial.

He showed a brief interest in flying and built his own aeroplane. It wasn't altogether successful. The plane did take off for a few minutes, but soon returned heavily to the ground.

Then Malcolm Campbell took to cars, owning a succession of them, each more powerful than the last.

At one time he had several cars to his name, and called his current racing model *Flapper*. But one day he saw Maeterlinck's opera *The Blue Bird*, and decided to rename all his cars *Bluebird* and paint them all blue. The names of Campbell and *Bluebird* were to remain synonymous with speed records for forty years.

His first record attempt was in 1922 when he broke the land speed record only to find that it could not be ratified because of the timing system he had used.

Then began a battle with the Americans. In 1924 and 1925 he set world speed records of 146.16 and 150.86 mph, only to lose the title almost immediately to other challengers.

By then he had become determined to keep the record in Britain. He had a new car built especially for the task, and again beat the existing record, only to have it taken a few weeks later by Segrave who reached 203.79 mph. The following year Malcolm Campbell secured the lead again, only to lose

the title to an American named Ray Keech.

In 1929 Segrave again recovered the title for Britain, and was knighted.

Between then and 1937, Campbell broke the record five more times raising it to 301.13 mph, and was knighted by King George V.

In 1937, having triumphed in the land speed records, Malcolm Campbell turned his attention to the water.

He had a hydroplane built, powered by a Rolls-Royce engine. He gave it the same name as his cars: *Bluebird*. In 1937 and 1938 he broke the record twice, his final speed being 130.93 mph.

Another new boat was built and

Left: November 1966: Donald Campbell pictured during a break in test trials on Lake Coniston, with Bluebird in the background.

Below: Malcolm Campbell on a test run in South Africa during a land speed attempt on Verneuk Pan. Bluebird achieved an average speed of 215 mph.

Land and Water

launched on to Coniston Water. At the launching ceremony was Donald Campbell, Malcolm's son.

The war brought an end to further attempts. After the war he looked into the possibility of converting the piston engine to jet. The results were not encouraging and as his health was not good he did not pursue the idea any further.

Malcolm Campbell died in 1948. His son Donald decided to keep up the family tradition of trying to beat speed records.

It took a lot of determination on his part to get started. Being the son of Malcolm Campbell meant that people were ready to accuse him of cashing in on his father's reputation. Then there was the ever-present problem of money. His father had had considerable financial security but Donald was to fight for years to overcome the problems of financing his record attempts—particularly as technical developments increased the costs.

If those factors were not enough to put him off, there was the added consideration that he had suffered from rheumatic fever as a child, and it had left him with a bad heart—bad enough for him to be rejected as unfit for military service.

But Donald Campbell had grit and courage and was not to be deterred by any problems. He had a long talk with Leo Villa, the brilliant engineer who had helped his father, and they decided that the old *Bluebird* was still good enough for a shot at the record.

At the first attempt they failed by 2 mph to break his father's old record. By June 1950 they were almost ready for another go, when they heard to their dismay that the Americans had just pushed the record speed up to 160.23 mph. They expected their boat to turn turtle at 160 mph, so they had to alter the design to counteract this. New propellers were installed and trials held in August. These were a disaster. After hearing strange noises they found that four cylinder heads were cracked and the hull damaged. The old R37 engine was a write-off.

Donald's optimism that the money for all the necessary repairs and alterations would be found somewhere luckily proved correct, thanks to the generosity of friends and large companies.

But disaster soon struck again. After a practice run of a magnificent 170 mph, the boat hit something submerged on the return journey and was a write-off.

The Americans again raised the record speed. Then in September 1952, John Cobb was killed on Loch Ness after achieving an unofficial 240 mph with his new jet-propelled boat *Crusader*.

This left Donald more determined than ever. A new boat was designed and built with jet engines and a metal body. In July 1955 Donald broke the record with a measured average over two runs of 202.32 mph.

He raised it twice more, finally reaching 225.63 mph in 1956. In May 1959 he finally beat the 250 mark when he averaged a speed of 260.35 mph.

He had started with the water speed record; now, like his father, he wanted both land and water records.

Donald Campbell was not a man to do things by halves. He had a car of really futuristic design built and he tried it out at Goodwood in July 1960. Then he took it to Utah to make a record attempt on the salt flats there. But the car hit a patch of wet, spongy salt, lost its adhesion and became airborne for 1000 feet. Over and over it went, sliding another 2000 feet before coming to a halt. Donald suffered serious injuries including a fracture to the base of the skull, a burst eardrum and severe lacerations. Only a miracle kept him alive.

The car was unusable, but Sir Alfred Owen offered to build him another one.

A few minor modifications were made to the previous design, and the new car was ready for trials by 1963. Two years earlier Donald had searched for a better trial area than Utah and found it in Lake

Land and Water

Not content with that, he took *Bluebird* boat to Lake Dumbleyung near Perth within weeks of his success at Lake Eyre, and broke his own water speed record with a run of 276.33 mph. He had achieved a truly fantastic double.

Still he was not satisfied. In 1966, at 46 years of age, he took the boat back to Coniston to try to break the magic 300 plus barrier. There were a number of problems to be solved, modifications to be made, but finally in January 1967 he set off for a record attempt. Conditions were good. The timekeepers took up their positions. The first run clocked up a speed of 297 mph. So far so good. He need only achieve 303 mph on the way back, and the target of an average 300 mph would be his.

He set off on the return journey only six minutes after completing the first run. The wash from the first run had not had time to settle and the officials were taken by surprise. Donald put his foot hard down and the boat started to seesaw violently. Just before the end of the marked mile the boat became airborne. She climbed into the air for about fifty feet at a steep angle, almost standing on her tail. Then she rolled over and crashed to the water. After floating for a few minutes she sank. Donald Campbell's body was never found. Unofficial timings suggested that he had achieved a speed of 328 mph.

Eyre in Australia. This was to be the scene of the next attempt. But it was not to be in 1963. Donald Campbell was ready, the car was ready and track had been prepared. But rains came unexpectedly after nearly ten years of drought, and swamped the new track. He had to abandon the attempt until the following year.

Unfortunately some of his backers were not so keen. The fiasco of 1963 had left him with little enthusiasm for further attempts and he had some difficulty in finding financial support.

To add to his dismay an American car broke the land speed record with a speed of 407.45 mph. It was disallowed because the car did not meet the correct specifications, but

Below: 4 January 1967: Donald Campbell and *Bluebird* flash aross Lake Coniston in a fatal bid to break their own world water speed record. Then tragedy struck. *Bluebird* soared into the air and hung there for seven seconds, before crashing back into the water. Above: Spray shoots into the air as *Bluebird* hits the lake.

the American success still left Donald with a sour feeling.

A new track was built at Lake Eyre, at right angles to the old. Finally on 17 July 1964 he took *Bluebird* out for an attempt at the record, and achieved a speed of 403.1 mph. He had made it. He had broken the record and the 400 mph barrier. Now he was the holder of both the land and water speed records.

Sporting Danger

Jump Jockey

There is one sport where the competitor *knows* that sooner or later he will be injured, possibly not once, but many times, and that sport is National Hunt racing.

There are more than 40 National Hunt courses in Great Britain, all of them different in character and many of them exceedingly difficult to ride. The ultimate test is the Grand National course at Aintree—four and a half miles with 30 thorn fences, many of them more than five feet high. The infamous Becher's Brook, with a 12-foot drop, is known to everybody, even non-racing enthusiasts.

Yet there are more jockeys trying to make a name in steeplechasing than there are horses for them to ride.

What makes them do it?

It isn't the money. The riding fee is often under £20, and a winning jockey also gets a percentage of the prize money, but only a handful of top jockeys earn as much as £10,000 a year.

It isn't the soft nature of the job. In 1975, 111 jockeys were sufficiently badly injured to claim compensation from the special fund set aside for them. Forty-five of them had broken legs, ribs, arms and collarbones.

Brian Fletcher, a brilliant rider perhaps best known for his Grand National win on Red Rum, retired at 29; Noel Flanagan at 28. In both cases, doctors advised that their bodies could not take much more.

Ken White had to pack up at 33; Macer Gifford at 32 had to face the fact that the accumulative effects of concussion meant his future lay in farming, not horse racing; Michael Eddery lost a leg; Colin Jackson ended up in a wheelchair; Tim Brookshaw finally managed to get around after spending many months in a wheelchair. And Tommy Stack, who had a magnificent win on Red Rum in the 1977 Grand National, was in a wheelchair only a few weeks later, fighting to get back on his feet in time for the 1978 race.

So, why do they do it? Top jockey John Francome has the answer: "When you're 'wasting' (having to lose weight) and out training in a chilly dawn, you long to have a job in a warm factory. But when you're the rider of a winner on a fine, spring afternoon, there's absolutely nothing else you'd rather be or do."

Aintree's Becher's Brook is legendary for the toll of horses and riders it takes each year in the Grand National. Left: A pile-up at Becher's in the '74 National. Below: Golden Rapper and jockey Johnny Francome come to grief at Becher's in '76.

Sporting Danger
Ballooning

On 27 August 1972 two press men from the *Daily Mirror*, Bill Marshall and Eric Piper, set off from Interlaken in Switzerland in what was then the world's largest balloon. Their departure was watched by large crowds of excited spectators. Their aim was to re-enact the balloon flight over the Swiss Alps into Italy made sixty years previously by a writer-photographer, Amande Console. However, they were forced down by bad weather when only three miles from the Italian border, and were rescued by a Swiss rescue helicopter.

Eric Piper is here seen using a remote control camera on the end of a pole.

Long before the Wright Brothers invented a practical aeroplane man had taken to the air in balloons, but with the advent of planes and airships the balloon disappeared as a means of flying.

Now, in the latter half of the 20th century, ballooning is back in popularity as a hobby and sport.

And modern balloonists are attempting dare-devil feats of which the pioneers could be proud.

For instance, *Motorway,* an AX 77 class Thunder hot-air balloon, raced another similar balloon across the Channel in July 1976. The balloons started from Barham, near Canterbury, and, although they landed four miles apart in France, they crossed the French coast at exactly the same time.

A bigger adventure still was planned by Karl Thomas, a 27-year-old German-American who attempted to be the first balloonist to cross the Atlantic. He took off from Lakehurst, New Jersey in his helium-filled balloon, but almost immediately had radio trouble.

When nothing was heard from him, search planes were sent out and hunted in vain for three days.

The crew of the Russian merchant ship *Dekabrisk* had probably never heard of Karl Thomas, but as their ship ploughed through the waves some three hundred miles off Bermuda, they saw a speck in the water.

There, sitting comfortably on his safety raft, was the missing balloonist. Karl *did* cross the Atlantic, but in the Russian ship.

History was made on 17 August 1978 when the three-man crew of the American balloon *Double Eagle II,* Larry Newman, Max Anderson and Ben Abruzzo, completed the first flight across the Atlantic from the United States to France.

Bullfighting

Aficionados!

Such is the Spanish passion for bullfighting that the officials at the bullrings have to keep a constant watch to prevent *aficionados* from jumping into the arena to fight the bulls. These *aficionados* are young men who want to demonstrate their own courage and, perhaps, get the chance to become professional bullfighters. But the dangers are so great even for the trained matadors, that the young *aficionados* are hustled out of the ring before they kill themselves.

Left: It is the matador who finally kills the bull. The graceful movements he makes as he plays the bull with his red cape are almost balletic. Bullfighting is the Spanish passion.

The slightly-built man in the glittering costume waves a red flannel close to the eyes of the bull. The bull does not see it and by instinct lurches forward. Has the bull been blinded, as the picadors insist? Or is it a long-sighted bull?

The man moves away from the bull to a distance at which, if it is long-sighted, it will see him.

The bull charges. . . .

Calmly the bullfighter awaits him. With the bull on top of him the man makes a 'pass' with the flannel to turn the bull away—a move he has performed so many times and with so much accuracy.

But the bull does not see it, pounds blindly on, drives a horn into the bullfighter's thigh and tosses him high into the air. The man comes down—right on to the bull's horns.

Thus died Joselito, King of the Matadors. He was only 25 years old.

In the recorded history of bullfighting, about 500 bullfighters have died at the hands, or rather the horns, of angry bulls.

When the bull goes into the ring he is faced not with one man, but many. First comes a team of banderillos on foot, to plant darts in the bull's back and tire him; next come the picadors on horseback to torment the bull with pikes; finally the matador comes into the ring to thrill the crowd with his passes with the cape, and to kill the bull with an elegant sword-thrust through the head.

Each bull is different. No matter how experienced the matador may be, he still has to study each bull, try to guess how he will react. And the penalty for guessing wrongly is injury or death.

So frequent are the accidents in the bullring that each major ring is equipped with its own hospital with full emergency facilities and doctors standing by.

But the doctors could not save Manolete, one of the most famous matadors there has ever been. Famed for his courage and for the grace with which he exercised his skill, Manolete was known and loved throughout the world. But on 28 August 1947 he thrust his sword into a bull which turned and inflicted a sharp blow on the Cordoban matador. Despite an operation and several blood transfusions, he died a few hours later.

The Running of the Bulls

A stampeding mass of bulls and men pounds through the streets of Pamplona each year. For one day, houses are boarded up and the townspeople stay safely behind fences or in the upper storeys as the bulls are driven through the streets towards the bullring.

To the young men, it is an irresistible challenge to show their courage. They join in the mad rush of bulls, the bravest being the one who stays closest to the bulls without being gored.

Incredibly enough, there are usually few serious casualties, though there are plenty of young men in Pamplona who can show the typical long, curved scar left by a bull's horn.

Sporting Danger

Acapulco Diving

Acapulco is perhaps best known as a playground for millionaires. But it has also made its name as the place where famous divers take off from rocks over a hundred feet high to splash into the sea far below. Tourists pay them just a few dollars a time to see them perform this feat!

Snowmobiling

Fancy motoring on skis? Then try snowmobiling, one of America's newest sports. Negotiating the bends can cause problems, but a skilful driver can counteract the sideways movement like a motorcyclist.

Ski Jumping

Ski jumpers are judged not only by the amount of ground they cover in one leap, but also by the style with which they carry out the jump. The skier has to pay great attention to the position of his body, hands and feet. Even a small error will lose him points. At the point of take-off the slope for which he is aiming seems far, far below!

Sporting Danger

Powerboat Racing

They're off! Streaking away down the Solent from the Isle of Wight are some of the 42 competitors in the 1969 Round-Britain powerboat race. The eventual winner was a man normally seen behind the wheel of a car —Finnish rally driver, Timo Makinen. After his triumph Timo said, "I like driving on water as much as I do on land." His boat, *Avenger Too*, covered 1403 gruelling miles before thundering home into Portsmouth at the end of the race.

Parachute Jumping

Leaping from an aircraft flying at 12,000 feet, is the sort of thing few people would contemplate. But for the Falcons, the RAF Parachute Display Team, it's all in a day's work. From left to right you can see the Team Leader, Flying Officer Geoffrey Greenland, Sgt. Joe Featherstone and Flt. Sgt. Terry Allen.

Sporting Danger
The Most Dangerous Sport?

Devotees of hang gliding say that it fulfils the dream which earth-bound man has always had of flying free like a bird. It is one of the fastest growing sports, having come to England from the United States where it is known by the more graceful name of sky-sailing.

The hang glider is really a very large, man-carrying kite. The experienced flyer can make it respond to his smallest movement, producing true flight freedom.

They usually take off from a hillside—or even a cliff top—and glide down to earth. Many people, including Members of Parliament, have claimed that it is the most dangerous of all the sports, and many people have already been severely injured or killed while practising.

The Southern Hang Gliding Club, with 250 members, defends its sport strongly, claiming that it is no more dangerous than a lot of other sports, such as skiing, where you also crash if you make a mistake.

"The trouble is," said one of their members, "that with any growth sport there are a large number of novices compared with experienced pilots. It is the novice who is most at risk."

Why do they do it? According to the hang-gliding pilots it is for the fantastic exhilaration of being aloft.

"It is a cross between flying a glider and going surfing," said 26-year-old John Ivers. "But it's not really an experience you can describe to someone who hasn't done it."

Above: Hang gliding? Some people always take things a little too far!

Snake Sacking

Among the more bizarre and rare sports of the world is snake sacking. Popular in Arizona and such out-of-the-way places, the reason for its lack of general popularity is not hard to find. The winner is the competitor who manages to get the most rattlesnakes into a sack in the shortest time!

The world record is five rattle-snakes into a sack in 18.3 seconds.

Some of the rules are unconsciously humorous. For instance: "All snakes must be unharmed. The penalty for injuring a snake is disqualification. If the snake bites either itself or the sacker, a five second penalty is added to the sacker's time."

Always supposing, of course, that the sacker is still conscious enough to be interested.

Bear Wrestling

Bear wrestling enjoyed a brief period of popularity in the United States during the last century.

The man responsible was himself a wrestler, Emil Regnier, who opened a beer shop in New York City in the 1870s. He decided to increase trade by holding wrestling matches in a tiny building known as the Athletic Hall, which was next to his shop.

It was in this hall, on 11 December 1877, that bear wrestling was launched as a professional sport.

The evening began with a conventional match between two men. Then the two bears were introduced into the contest.

One sat on his haunches while the other did a little dance. Then another wrestler, William Heyster, known as The Oak of the Rhine, proceeded to square off against the large bear which, like his smaller companion, was muzzled and had had his foreclaws filed.

Heyster found the bear immovable. Much as he tried to throw the bear to the ground, the obstinate creature resisted. Since the bear showed no desire to throw Heyster, the bout fizzled out in a draw.

Regnier himself tackled the smaller bear with slightly better results. Both fell to the ground and, presumably because the bear did not know the rules,

Regnier was able to roll the animal on to its back and was thus declared the winner.

The spectacle was exciting enough to attract audiences, and other bouts were staged in other halls.

The star performers were Regnier (human) and Lena (a bear). Lena showed an aptitude for wrestling and even defeated Regnier in one bout.

A troupe of bears and wrestlers was formed and went on a tour of the United States.

But disaster struck. Lena grabbed a wrestler named Jean Francis Borne and squeezed him until he collapsed. He died later, and bear wrestling went into a decline from which it never recovered.

The Entertainers

Houdini

The most famous of all the escapologists is undoubtedly the Great Houdini. He made a world-wide reputation for himself by escaping from all manner of seemingly impossible situations. One of his most famous tricks was to free himself from a strait-jacket while suspended by his feet high above the crowd.

Another escape which made audiences gasp was to release himself from a locked box which had been submerged in water.

Born Erik Weisz in Budapest, Hungary, in 1874, Houdini's first public appearances were as an acrobat. In 1900 he began to specialise in escapology and soon built up a reputation. He appeared in many top theatres and also performed in the open air where he could be seen by thousands of people at a time. On a few occasions he appeared in early motion pictures.

Houdini was a trained athlete and champion swimmer, and it was his superb fitness that enabled him to perform his remarkable escapes. He could hold his breath under water for long periods and had excellent muscular control.

Unfortunately it was this that led to his death in 1926. He claimed—rightly—that he could withstand a severe blow to the stomach. A young student took him at his word and hit him unexpectedly, not realising that Houdini needed time to prepare himself to withstand the blow. Houdini died from peritonitis resulting from a ruptured appendix.

Right: Hungarian-born Harry Houdini, the greatest of all the escapologists, performing a water tank trick, shackled and locked in. He escaped from the tank in an amazing three and a half minutes!

The Entertainers
The Circus

The audience at a circus is there not only to be entertained and thrilled but also to be frightened by the performance. Those who work in the circus are well aware of this, and realise that it is only by attempting more and more daring feats that they can hope to make a name for themselves. People like fire-eater Judy Allen take enormous risks in order to provide entertainment. Of her act she says, "It's no trick. Basically it's getting used to it and not being frightened."

For lion tamer Mike Sheedy, the picture shows him in action on his own with the lions for the very first time. Previously he had always been supervised in the cage, but

Right: Showgirl Judy Allen demonstrates how easy it is to be a fire-eater. Judy uses special lighted torches in her act, which she then puts in her mouth or around her body.

Below: Mr Collins used to throw knives at his wife for a living. Mrs Collins lies on a revolving wheel while her husband prepares to aim. She has since retired from the act after 21 years.

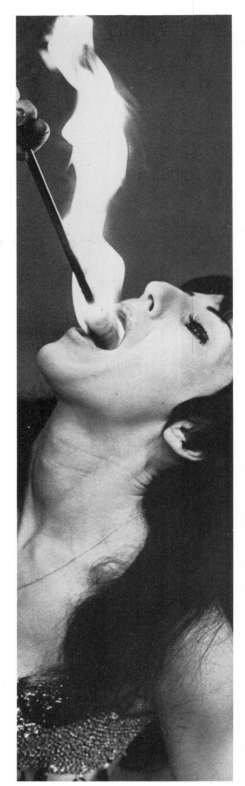

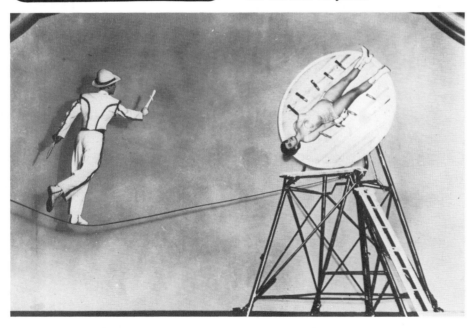

after five months of training, he was allowed to take complete charge. For the 33-year-old former lorry driver, it was a dream come true.

One of elephant trainer Yasmine Smart's favourite friends was the elephant Burma. She loved Burma, and despite his gigantic size she was confident that he would not harm her. Yasmine, a daughter of circus people, was just one of the children who spend all their spare time in the ring, practising for the time when they can become part of the show.

It isn't animals that Agnes Collins has to trust, but her own father. She lies on a revolving wheel while her father throws knives at her. If that sounds hair-raising—don't forget that her father is standing on one leg on a slack rope as he throws! In the picture is Agnes's mother Elizabeth, who gave up the job after 21 years in the act. And in that time she was not even nicked by a knife.

Above: Lion trainer Mike Sheedy was a lorry driver until the circus came to town. Now, in the lions' cage, Mike faces up to Romeo.

Below: Yasmine Smart, now a famous elephant trainer, showed her love and trust of elephants even at 10 years old, as Burma walked over her.

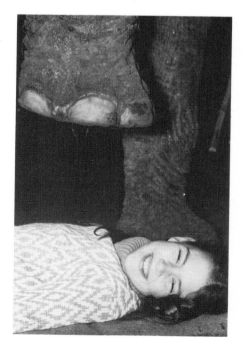

Secrets of a Circus Star

The man seen on page 114 diving full-length through a ring of gleaming, razor-sharp knives is Jos de Graff. Jos, who comes from Holland, is concerned that children, after seeing his act, may try to imitate him. So—to prevent any accidents, he was prepared to reveal his secret! First of all you have to get the jump exactly right by pacing out the approach. "And when you practise the dives, you use a hoop of *rubber* knives," Jos explained. "One slip of the foot when you take off and the result would be fatal." This isn't the only trick Jos performs using sword blades—he also walks up a ladder fitted with knife-edge steps!

The Entertainers
Escapology

Escaping from a burning box is 17-year-old Paul Randall's way of making money. He did it for a £50 bet after hearing that another man had been seriously burned attempting the same trick.

Paul was handcuffed, padlocked into a mailbag and nailed into the wooden box. A huge bonfire was lit over the box, and ninety seconds later Paul emerged, hot under the collar but only slightly singed. He admitted afterwards that it had been more difficult than he had expected. "The worst part was when I kicked the box open and the flames were sucked in," he said.

Paul, a part-time illusionist, refused to give away the secret of performing the trick successfully. "That's a trade secret," he said.

Just Hanging Around

A crowd took time off from its Christmas shopping in December 1963 to gaze up at Rita Roeber, a trapeze artist from Holland, as she dangled 80 feet above the ground. Rita couldn't resist the challenge when she saw a giant crane towering over a building site in the middle of Leeds. She donned her circus costume and proceeded to practise her act. Far below, her father, ex-trapeze artist Max Roeber, watched anxiously as Rita performed her specialities—from the upside-down splits to hanging by one leg. The only time he called to her to stop was when she was preparing to hang by her toes!

Her only comment when she touched earth again was: "It was so cold."

The Entertainers

Snake Charmer

The Indian seen charming his snakes from their basket is continuing an ancient Indian tradition. The snakes are 'charmed' by the sound of the instrument he is playing—a kind of pipe—and are hypnotised by the music. Some charmers wear a glittering gem on their fingers, which is also supposed to attract and hypnotise the snakes. Different sorts of snakes can be used, but cobras, like the ones in the picture, are the best. They create a dramatic effect as they rise from the basket with their 'hoods' spread behind their heads, and 'dance' for the charmer.

Left: Escapologist Alan Alan believes in living dangerously. For this stunt he was suspended upside down, handcuffed and padlocked, from the top of a 100-foot crane. Then the rope from which he hung was soaked in petrol and set on fire. Alan had just three minutes to extricate himself!

Below: Mike Costello (alias Blondini) climbs into a box wired up with enough dynamite to wreck a three-storey building, and his wife Sally presses the button! As the smoke clears, Mike crawls out—usually unhurt but for a splitting headache! Two other men who tried the trick died in the attempt.

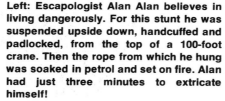

The Entertainers
Evel Knievel

Evel Knievel, who was born in Butte, Montana in 1939 as Robert Craig Kennedy, became famous throughout the world for his daring stunts, and broke many bones in his body. But perhaps the stunt that aroused the most publicity was in September 1974 when he announced that he was going to jump across Snake River Canyon, Idaho, U.S.A., which measures roughly 1600 feet across. For the attempt he had developed a special steam-powered Sky Cycle. This is a kind of missile with a cockpit which was supposed to reach a speed of 200 mph as it went up a runway 108 ft long. The landing on the other side was to be achieved by a drag chute on the sky cycle and a shock absorber in the nose.

In the event, the attempt ended dismally. The cycle took off and then floated gently—and safely —into the canyon on a parachute. Because of the advance publicity, the stunt was estimated to have grossed over 30 million dollars, of which Evel Knievel received 13 million dollars, making him the highest paid entertainer in the world.

It's Just an Illusion . . .

Risking their lives to enthrall an audience is an everyday event to many entertainers, and usually their stunts come off successfully. But not always.

One of the unlucky ones was Chung Ling Soo, the illusionist. His name was not really Chung Ling Soo—he was actually an Englishman named William Robinson—but for years everybody thought he was Chinese. He

The Entertainers

Left: Here's one man who really does go to work on an egg! The circus performer seen here frying up a meal in a hurry is fire-eater Ataualpa. In an emergency he can always double up as a cook—and supply his own power. And his act can truly be said to be one of the hottest things in the circus!

Below: Passers-by seem not to have noticed this man balancing on top of the roof of the Royal Garden Hotel, Kensington, in London. So, as the people below go about their daily business, circus trapeze artist Sebastian unconcernedly flexes his muscles—200 feet up!

employed a Korean to help him and to act as his interpreter. So clever were they at chattering to each other in pidgin English that not even the stage hands realised he was not Chinese.

Chung Ling Soo's most dramatic illusion was to catch on a plate near his chest bullets which were fired at him by the Korean. Real bullets were handed to members of the audience who initialled them before the rifle was loaded. But the rifle used by the Korean assistant was fitted with an automatic device which collected the live bullets as they were fed into it, and then dropped blanks into the magazine in their place.

One night at the Wood Green Empire, the automatic device failed. William Robinson, alias Chung Ling Soo, fell dead to the floor with real bullets in his chest.

That night there was no illusion. . . .

The Search for Oil

Red Adair

One of the most amazing men in the world of oil excavation is the Texan Red Adair. When there is serious trouble on a rig, particularly when there has been a dangerous 'blow-out' and fire is raging round it, Red Adair and his team of experts are called upon to take on the extremely hazardous task of stopping the flames and capping the well.

It takes enormous courage to face the might of an oil well that is effectively out of control. Red Adair's fees are high, but the oil companies know that he is worth it.

But there can be more at stake than just the lost oil. In 1977, Red Adair was called to the Ekofisk field in the North Sea. There had been a massive blow-out and thousands of tonnes of oil were spewed into the sea, creating a mammoth slick that threatened to cause an ecological disaster.

Thanks to the courage and skill of Red Adair, the leak was plugged before too much damage was done.

North Sea Oil

A tanker being loaded with oil from the Exposed Location Single Buoy Mooring (ELSBM for short!) in the Auk oilfield in the North Sea. Oil flows from the Auk production platform along a 2km pipeline. The tankers (as shown in the picture) are then fed with their cargoes of oil through a flexible hose mounted on a reel in the ELSBM—a kind of North Sea petrol pump for oil tankers!

The Search for Oil
Diving for Oil

Man is constantly searching for new supplies of energy. For centuries he has dug coal out of the mines to produce gas and electricity. Oil has been found in large oil wells mainly in America and the Middle East.

But one of the most important of the recent discoveries for Western Europe was the presence of vast quantities of natural gas and oil underneath the North Sea.

The problem was—how to get it out? The North Sea is notoriously rough and it required great physical courage to brave the dangers of excavating and searching for the hidden energy.

The sea is basically a hostile environment for Man. Underwater exploration has always been extremely dangerous because the diver is completely dependent on life support systems to enable him to breathe. Even these have a limited use: for instance a diver in an aqualung can't stay under water for very long and can't go down to great depths.

In addition, the diver has always had to face the danger of 'the bends'. While he is under water, the pressure causes gases to be absorbed into his system, and if these are not released slowly the diver can suffer from 'the bends', which cause severe pain and can even kill him.

It was obvious that if North Sea oil and gas were to be exploited to the full, new ways of staying under water would have to be found. Previous methods of exploring the bottom of the sea had been aimed at men making scientific surveys or studying marine life. North Sea oil rig divers would have to be able to perform heavy tasks of construction under water and carry out the same sort of manual labour as workers on land.

The first need was to find some way of enabling divers to stay under water for longer periods. Until recently, a diver might spend only a short time on the sea bed, only a short time 'depressurizing' afterwards. Submarines made it possible for men to stay under the sea for months at a time, but there were too many tasks which could not be performed from the inside of a submarine. There was no substitute for the diver.

Jacques Cousteau designed a house which he called *Diogenes*, a complete home beneath the sea with beds, shower, heating and cooking facilities. Men could live in *Diogenes* and work from there without having to surface. Since then there have been many devel-

Above: A 'roughneck' wrestling with the drill stem on a semi-submersible drilling platform. Right: A 'roughneck' on the BP oil rig 120 miles off Aberdeen, in Scotland.

opments in undersea living, with both the Americans and the French building small, underwater 'villages'. They have found that it is easy to communicate with each other under water, and that hard physical labour can be easier beneath the sea than on land.

But villages on the sea bed are really for the future. Now, the divers around the oil rigs have to surface regularly. One of the techniques which has been perfected over recent years is to keep the diver under pressure for up to a month. After surfacing from the dive, the diver lives and sleeps in a pressure chamber on the surface ready to make a further succession of dives; he does not depressurize until his spell of work is finished.

The casualty rate for divers is high, but without their skill the North Sea oil rigs would not be able to function.

However, it is not only the divers who take risks. Everybody who works on an oil rig is to some extent taking a risk.

Among the most dangerous jobs on the oil rig is that of a 'roughneck'. 'Roughnecks' are the men who do most of the difficult, physical work on the rig. They need a good head for heights as they often have to work many feet above the deck, perched precariously with only a safety harness to support them.

The oil rigs have to be completely self-supporting in terms of stocks of food and equipment. Constant rough weather can hamper deliveries and make life even tougher for the oil men.

If conditions become too dangerous on the rig, for instance when the weather is really appalling, they rely on the helicopter service (see page 57) to bring them safely to dry land.

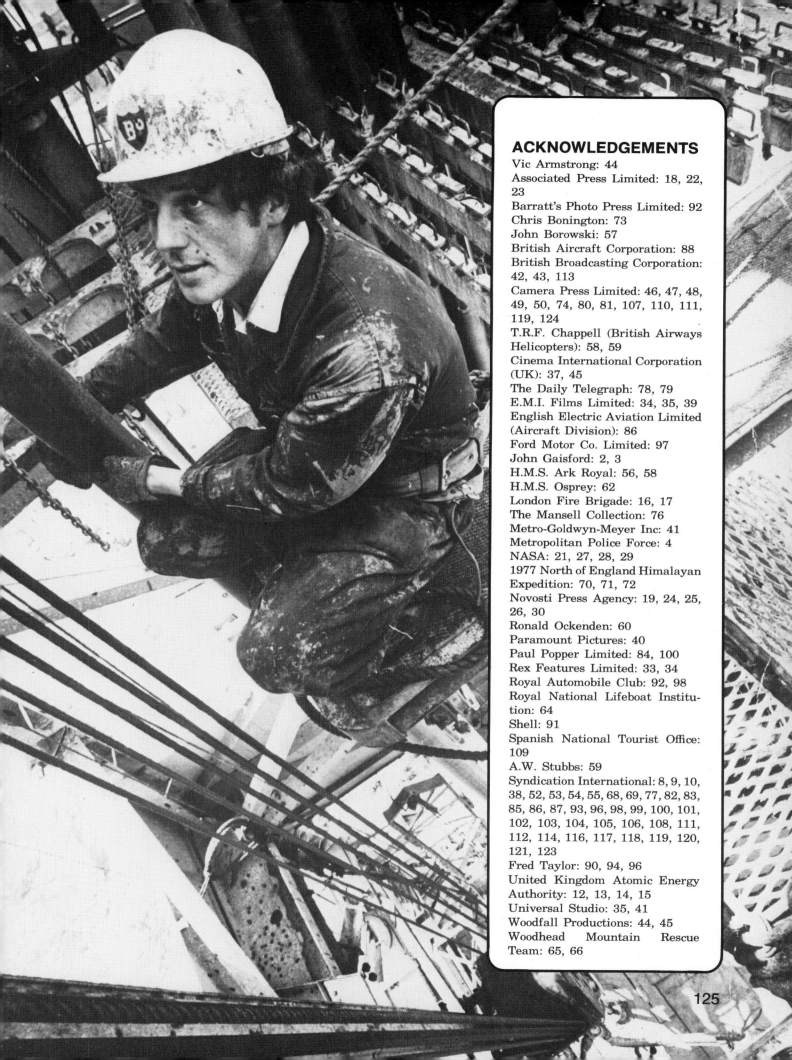

ACKNOWLEDGEMENTS

Vic Armstrong: 44
Associated Press Limited: 18, 22, 23
Barratt's Photo Press Limited: 92
Chris Bonington: 73
John Borowski: 57
British Aircraft Corporation: 88
British Broadcasting Corporation: 42, 43, 113
Camera Press Limited: 46, 47, 48, 49, 50, 74, 80, 81, 107, 110, 111, 119, 124
T.R.F. Chappell (British Airways Helicopters): 58, 59
Cinema International Corporation (UK): 37, 45
The Daily Telegraph: 78, 79
E.M.I. Films Limited: 34, 35, 39
English Electric Aviation Limited (Aircraft Division): 86
Ford Motor Co. Limited: 97
John Gaisford: 2, 3
H.M.S. Ark Royal: 56, 58
H.M.S. Osprey: 62
London Fire Brigade: 16, 17
The Mansell Collection: 76
Metro-Goldwyn-Meyer Inc: 41
Metropolitan Police Force: 4
NASA: 21, 27, 28, 29
1977 North of England Himalayan Expedition: 70, 71, 72
Novosti Press Agency: 19, 24, 25, 26, 30
Ronald Ockenden: 60
Paramount Pictures: 40
Paul Popper Limited: 84, 100
Rex Features Limited: 33, 34
Royal Automobile Club: 92, 98
Royal National Lifeboat Institution: 64
Shell: 91
Spanish National Tourist Office: 109
A.W. Stubbs: 59
Syndication International: 8, 9, 10, 38, 52, 53, 54, 55, 68, 69, 77, 82, 83, 85, 86, 87, 93, 96, 98, 99, 100, 101, 102, 103, 104, 105, 106, 108, 111, 112, 114, 116, 117, 118, 119, 120, 121, 123
Fred Taylor: 90, 94, 96
United Kingdom Atomic Energy Authority: 12, 13, 14, 15
Universal Studio: 35, 41
Woodfall Productions: 44, 45
Woodhead Mountain Rescue Team: 65, 66